BETTY WHITE:
THE FIRST 90 YEARS

Andrew E. Stoner

Blue River Press

ISBN-13: 978-1-935628-23-1
Cover Design: Phil Velikan
Cover Photos: Betty White, Phil Stafford / Shutterstock.com; *The
Mary Tyler Moore Show* Cast, Associated Press / Reed Saxon.
Layout/Design: MaryKay Hruskocy Scott, Candor Creative, LLC
Proofreader: David Ruiz del Vizo, MADA Writing Services

Printed in the United States of America
10 9 8 7 6 5 4 3 2 1

Blue River Press, Indianapolis, Indiana
Distributed by Cardinal Publishers Group
Tom Doherty Company, Inc.
www.cardinalpub.com

For Betty, Bea, Rue and Estelle . . . thanks for the memories.

Table of Contents

Preface

It's worth noting right up front, I've never met Betty White (although I've wanted to for a long time), and she doesn't know who the heck I am. But then again, that's the way it is for millions of us who feel we *know* Betty on a very personal level, even those of us who have never been in her presence.

We feel this special love and affection that runs as deep as the dimples adorning Betty's lovely smile; and she fulfills without question, for many of us, the role of beloved aunt, cousin or even grandmother. She's that fun person you are hoping you will see at the reunion; and the one you make a special effort to sit near.

Betty's fans—all of us old timers who knew her and her work before she was Rose or Elka, and the new ones who think she's that "funny old lady" from *The Proposal*—greet her in our hearts and minds in a way we reserve for really special folk. It's an amazing contrast to Betty's personal life, which she often reminds people is one where she prefers time alone, and enjoys the company of her dogs as much as she does any special person. Make no mistake, Betty is not lonely—after all, she can command an in-person or on- screen crowd with the snap of a finger.

When I started this work, I so hoped to interview or meet Miss White. It was a long-term goal that has yet to come to pass—I'm still hopeful that we one day may meet. But the decision to go ahead and share memories about Betty and her amazing career was an easy one. It's as if you were to ask me to open up my scrapbook and tell you all about my favorite star, Betty White. I'd be more than happy to do so!

And so, that's really what this book is. A glimpse into the incredible life and career of Betty White through the lens of a loving fan that has plenty of company in the front row in the Betty White Admiration Society. I've spent considerable time exploring Betty's early career, including her truly pioneering involvement in some of America's earliest television telecasts, to her long-term and deep commitment to animals and our environment.

But lest you worry this is a textbook—it is not. There is plenty of fun here, from the incredible zingers Betty's character Sue Ann Nivens used to deliver on *The Mary Tyler Moore Show* to the feather-brained but loving outlook of Rose Nylund from *The Golden Girls*. And of course, there's a retracing of an incredible late-life resurgence that has cast her as one of the most beloved and funniest actresses out there—whether you're 16 or 60.

My hope is that you will enjoy this trip down memory lane about Betty's life—written with no objectivity at all—written by a true fan that is forever grateful for the countless moments in life Betty has filled with laughter and love. Whether you call her "America's Sweetheart" or "America's Golden Girl,"; whatever you do, you cannot forget the incomparable Miss Betty White!

Andrew E. Stoner
November 2012

Betty took home a Lifetime Achievement Award from the Screen Actors Guild Awards in January 2010, and just a year later was back as the winner as Outstanding Female in a Comedy Series for her work on *Hot in Cleveland*. During the 2010 awards, co-star Sandra Bullock paid a moving and hilarious tribute to her friend Betty. *(Featureflash/Shutterstock.com)*

1

SENIOR MOMENTS

WHO NEEDS A COMEBACK?

Convinced that everyone else was preoccupied with how old they were, as Betty White entered her 90th year she adopted a grateful, and of course, humorous mantra. "I'm the luckiest broad on two feet," she declared.[1]

That she's enjoyed 90 years of life is not that unexpected—her own mother lived 86 years—but that she's as big a star as there is after nine decades of life and more than six decades in show business in saying something. Perhaps only George Burns, who died in 1996 at the age of 100, could boast a bigger and longer longevity in the hearts and minds of America.

The key to Betty's health and longevity? Not the diet a doctor would recommend: Betty loves hot dogs and Red Vines licorice candy. "I should follow better eating health rules," Betty admits. "But hot dogs and Red Vines and potato chips and French fries are my favorite foods." It's hard to argue with her approach, however, as she declares herself "good and energetic" and adds,

"There's no spare time, so I'm active all the time. I think that forces you to stay well. To be 90 . . . and still be working, that's what I wouldn't have expected."[2]

Betty's routine, by the way, includes no formal exercise program. Instead, she said she relies on her bad memory which she says forces all sorts of trips up and down the stairs in her two-story home.

The issue of whether Betty has actually had a late career comeback, or has always been there is one that keeps coming up. CNN commentator Piers Morgan asked Betty during his interview about her alleged "comeback" to celebrity status. Betty's take: Come back from what? She's always been there. Betty's been a part of American TV life for almost as long as most of us have been alive. For a star as big as Betty, literally *never* off television for any extended period for the first half century of television broadcasting, a comeback was unneeded. One doesn't need to come back to a presence on TV that is as natural as the medium itself.

"Everybody says, 'So nice to see you back,'" Betty said. "I've never been away, guys. I've been working for 63 years."[3]

BETTY'S SENIOR MOMENTS

Perhaps it is the security of all those years in TV provides, but with her popularity secured, in 2012 Betty broke new ground and shed her personal rule about airing her political views. In addition to taping a TV ad in support of a Democratic candidate for Congress in southern California, Betty openly declared her support for the re-election of President Barack Obama. Betty says she normally likes to act in a bi-partisan way for fear of turning off her fans, but says the 2012 election is important and she said she likes "how (Obama) represents us" and "very, very much favors" Obama for re-election. She later participated in a star-studded fundraiser for Obama in the Hollywood home of actor George Clooney that raised a reported $15 million for the Obama campaign.[4]

She also weighed in on the issue of gay marriage—a divisive issue for some—noting that she doesn't care who loves who, as long as they are good people. "I really don't care with whom you sleep," she says. "I just care about what kind of decent human being you are. I figure all the rest of it is your business and not mine."[5]

And while Betty's star was rising—or at least still shining as bright as ever (depending on whom you ask)—sharing the praise and the limelight came naturally for her, it's always been a part of Betty's personality. During earlier Emmy Awards broadcasts where she was nominated against co-stars Bea Arthur, Rue McClanahan and Estelle Getty for their work on *The Golden Girls*, it was Betty who would be clapping loudest when one of her pals won the big prize.

The same was true in 2012 when *Hot in Cleveland* co-star Valerie Bertinelli was awarded the 2,476th star on the Hollywood Walk of Fame. Betty was there, front and center, along with *Hot in Cleveland* co-stars Jane Leeves and Wendie Malick. Betty was beaming with pride for her younger co-star. "Val, dear, I am thrilled with this honor for you today and it really is an honor," she said. "Years and years, decades ago, when they were just trying to fill up those places, I got a star . . . they just wanted to fill up the sidewalk. But this is a real honor . . . so I hope you'll cherish this honor as we all do—we love to brag about it—'We know Valerie Bertinelli'—she is the dearest, she is the well-deserving and we love her so much."[6]

Bertinelli, along with everyone else associated with TV Land's franchise hit *Hot in Cleveland*, seem to understand they owe a bit of their rise to the incredible year Betty enjoyed starting in 2010, a year in which fans of the popular syndicated entertainment show *Extra* voted Betty their No. 5 top star for the year.

The year also saw Betty bring home her seventh Emmy award—out of 21 Emmy nominations during her career. The first woman to win an Emmy for hosting a game show, her 2010 win was for "Outstanding Guest Actress in a Comedy Series" for her appearance on *Saturday Night Live*. She won over some high-powered competition, including Jane Lynch for *Two and a Half Men*, Tina Fey for her guest hosting spot on *SNL*, Elaine Stritch for *30 Rock*, Kristin Chenoweth for *Glee*, Kathryn Joosten for *Desperate Housewives*, and Christine Baranski for *The Big Bang Theory*. The *2010 MTV Movie Awards* also recognized Betty's increased presence on the big screen, giving her an award titled the "Best WTF Moment."

To be precise, by 2010, Betty was hot.

A prime example: The much-anticipated June 2010 premier of her new made-for-cable-TV series, *Hot in Cleveland*, set a new viewership record for TV Land. The show drew 4.75 million viewers in its first week and was the most watched show ever for TV Land, a network dedicated to classic TV series and stars.[7]

Perhaps even more impressive—though hardly a network record—Betty successfully drew an 18-month high rating for NBC's sometimes faltering *Saturday Night Live*. Her Mother's Day 2010 appearance scored an 8.8 household rating—the highest since the show's last pre-2008 election special.[8]

Without a doubt, the success introduced Betty to a whole new generation of fans—21st century fans whose parents and grandparents have known Betty for decades. For all those young ones who think they have "discovered" this talented and funny lady, their parents and grandparents can tell them a story or two.

But Betty's successes—often playing against type as a smart-mouth, acid-tongued senior with a strong sex drive—really just reveals what her most loyal fans always knew: Betty possesses world class comedic timing and could make any audience laugh. Interestingly, it was the now defunct American Comedy Awards that proved that point to another new generation of fans just getting to know Betty.

Just two years into *The Golden Girls*, Betty faced off in the 1987 American Comedy Awards against co-stars Bea Arthur and Estelle Getty (Rue McClanahan was overlooked for a nomination) for "Best Female Performer in a Television Series." The category included much younger prime-time comedians of the era, Shelley Long on NBC's mega-hit *Cheers*, and Julia Duffy from CBS' *Newhart*. Regardless, Betty took home the trophy, and in accepting it, stole the show.

"Now this is a joke, right?" Betty asked to uproarious laughter. "This is a comedy show and this is just some kind of a put up, right? We'll put the old broad up here with an award, and then we'll take it away, right?"[9]

After offering one of her famous double-entendres: "the first time for anything is simply marvelous" she followed that up with a sung line from the song, "Try To Remember." But then Betty got serious.

"I am genuinely and deeply thrilled, but two other ladies (Bea and Estelle) deserve it every bit as much as me, and we share it, all of us," Betty said. "Estelle and Bea, thank you!"[10]

Whether the audience realized it or not, it was no easy task to be as relevant and as funny as Betty was throughout her career—even into her senior years—as the comedy award recognized.

Consider, the nature of comedy didn't change much over the years, but the audience changed dramatically over the course of Betty's career.

"The audience has changed. They're much more sophisticated. They've heard every joke and know every story line. That's a hard audience to surprise, and a hard audience to get a laugh from," Betty said.[11]

Commercial Success

Want more evidence of Betty's growing relevance to younger audiences? The 2010 Super Bowl on CBS was a prime example. The annual extravaganza generated a larger than average audience—many Americans excited about the prospects of the lowly New Orleans Saints, hailing from the hurricane-ravaged city of Louisiana, against the superstar Indianapolis Colts. But as usual, the game was only part of the attraction. Over the years as the Super Bowl has grown to be America's quintessential shared TV experience, and the advertisements played during the Super Bowl are equally valued.

Clearly the most "talked about" ad of the entire show was one produced by Mars Candy, the makers of the Snickers candy bar, called "Game." Directed by Craig Gillespie, "Game" featured Betty being tackled in the mud in a rough game of pick-up football. As she gets up from the hard hit, a teammate criticizes her "for playing like Betty White."

Betty has a great comeback, "That's not what your girlfriend told me last night."

Promptly, Betty's character eats a Snickers bar and returns to his regular self—a man—and the game goes on (but not before another TV legend, Abe Vigoda appears as the quarterback who gets sacked in the mud).

The ad won the coveted No. 1 spot on USA Today's "Super Bowl Ad Meter" from fans, but also won a commercial, primetime Emmy Award nomination. The pairing of the senior citizen (Betty White) and a heavy youth demographic show (the Super Bowl) yielded the Snickers bar advertising series its highest ratings in years, reported Shoot, an online advertising industry vehicle.[12]

The Snickers ad "speaks to the 20 to 25-year-old guy as well as to grandma and everybody else who is part of the Snickers' universe —(it) speaks to all ages as likeable and fun work," said David Lubars, one of the ad's producers.[13]

Lubars also noted what a good sport and "a hoot" Betty was to work with on producing the ad. She readily agreed to lie down in a mud puddle with the stunt man on top of her to create the effect of having been tackled. Lubars quoted Betty as saying, "I prefer it when the guy buys me drinks first."[14]

Betty acknowledges the ad is a classic—one people still talk about—but she credits the stunt woman who took the actual hit and landed in the mud puddle. "When we did the Snickers thing, it was early in the morning and it was cold and there was this pool of muddy water," she said. "I was out on the field playing football with a bunch of young guys, which I do every Saturday! But at this one point, the stunt woman has to take this drive into the muddy pool . . . she did the dive and I just laid down and I got the laugh. That's not fair!"[15]

To no one's surprise—Betty's connection to Snickers bars helped propel it to the nation's No. 1 spot among candy and gum items purchased. With sales of $3.57 billion in 2012, Snickers moved ahead of M&Ms and Trident gum to become the world's favorite confection.[16]

This wasn't the first time Betty had done commercials, but it was the most successful effort.

Earlier, more typical efforts included 1970s ads where she appeared as the frequent TV spokesperson for Spray 'n Wash stain remover. She also did ASPCA ads for the Latham Foundation.

In a 1970s era ad for Tyco blocks—a competitor with Lego—Betty touted them at a better price. "If you can't tell the difference, why pay the difference?" she asked. She proclaims that her race to find a bargain had won her the name "Picky White."

In 2012, Cincinnati-based Proctor & Gamble jumped on board and relaunched its venerable brand Tide and Tide Plus (with bleach) under a new name—"Tide Vivid White."

Betty's role? She's touting the product's ability to keep white clothes white via Facebook and TV ads. Under the theme, "Breaking the Rules of White" produced by ad agency Saatchi and Saatchi, the commercial is one of little risk. Who dislikes Betty? Anyone?

"We are thrilled to be working with Betty because she truly embodies the way we want people to feel when they trust their clothing to Tide Vivid White + Bright," said Raquel Rozas, a Proctor & Gamble spokeswoman. "People should be able to enjoy themselves and embrace wearing the color white without having to stick to self-imposed rules while wearing it."[17]

The Facebook component of the ad—that included a live chat with Betty and her fans—broke Betty's rule to stay off the social networking site after her ride atop the fan-driven movement for her to host *Saturday Night Live* in 2010.

"They came to me with the offer and I've had Tide under my sink for years," Betty said. "And with a name like 'White,' I thought Tide White and Bright was appropriate."[18]

In the ad, Betty says, "I know what you're thinking," as she points to her white outfit. "It's a hot white number, but what a hassle to care for—all that pretreating and chlorine bleach, and don't even think about working up a sweat in the club. That's my Tide and that's how I break the rules of White," Betty concludes.[19]

The ad was a success—as *New York Times* writer Andrew Adam Newman wrote, "Some advertising ideas seem to have a celebrity's name written all over them, but certainly that has never been as appropriate as it is for a new campaign for Tide Vivid White and Bright that stars Betty White."[20]

Newman also reported that according to Q Scores Company, an agency that tracks the popularity of more than 1,800 celebrities, Betty White is tied with Tom Hanks as having the highest favorability rating.

In 2011, Ipsos conducted a survey of more than 2,000 adults in the U.S. and found Betty at the top as the nation's favorite celebrity, with an 86 percent favorable rating. She edged out actors Denzel Washington and Sandra Bullock who came in at 85 and 84 percent, respectively. Betty's presence at the top of the list was no small task—the list contains some heavyweights— including Clint Eastwood, Tom Hanks, Harrison Ford, Kate Middleton, Morgan Freeman, Will Smith, and Johnny Depp.

Researchers didn't have to go to all that trouble and research though. Evidence of her popularity is seemingly everywhere. Betty's 2011 rap music video—"I'm Still Hot"— featuring scantily clad muscle men and electronic dance artist Luciana—has earned more than one million "hits" or views on the popular online site, YouTube.

A Facebook Phenomenon

YouTube is not the only social media indicator that Betty is hot. Facebook played a critical role in perhaps her greatest senior moments to date. More than 500,000 Facebook users eventually signed on, urging Lorne Michaels and the producers of NBC's *Saturday Night Live* to have Betty on as host.

"I'm a technological spazz," Betty said, admitting she doesn't have a Facebook account and rarely uses the computer at all. "People would tell me they saw this Facebook thing and all these people had joined. I couldn't believe it, and I thought they were putting me on."[21]

Betty said the Facebook phenomenon "came out of left field and I was astounded. I told my agent, please say, 'Thank you, but no thank you.' He said, 'You have to do it. If you don't do it, I'll divorce you.' I love my agent, so here I am doing it."[22]

Aware that the Facebook effort and the resulting publicity likely would deliver a large audience, Betty worried aloud about how good she would be on the live show since she does not work on camera from cue cards. "I memorize or ad lib," she said. "And I know with the changing scripts . . . that won't be possible. And with cue cards, I hope I don't have to wear my glasses. I hope the print is big enough. If it isn't, I'll do the show with my glasses."[23]

In the end, Betty did the show without her glasses—and did just fine. She was, in fact, spectacular.

Betty said she was open to whatever the producers and writers of *SNL* had in store for her, "All I know is that I have veto power if there's something I really don't want to do."[24]

Live from New York—It's Betty!

Mother's Day 2010 will always be remembered for the time when Facebook fans moved an entire network—NBC—to invite the one and only Betty to host its long-running late night comedy staple: *Saturday Night Live*.

The show was an instant hit among regular *SNL* fans and a whole new pack of followers.[25]

Long-term fans know, however, this was not Betty's first brush with *Saturday Night Live*. During a *Golden Girls* episode more than two decades earlier, under the influence of anesthesia for a pending operation, Betty's character Rose Nylund blurted out, "Live from New York! It's *Saturday Night*!"

Betty's monologue to open the show was a sign of the good stuff to follow. She noted this was not her first time to host a live TV show—reminding the audience that her early sitcom *Life with Elizabeth* was often performed live. "Back then we didn't want to do it live, we just didn't know how to tape things," she said. "So I don't know what this show's excuse is."[26]

She was quick to thank her Facebook fans for getting her the hosting gig. In her classic deadpan style, she noted, "When I first heard about the campaign to get me to host *Saturday Night Live*, I didn't know what Facebook was. And now that I do know what it is, I have to say, it sounds like a huge waste of time. I would never say people on it are losers, but that's only because I'm polite."[27]

Betty said younger friends had told her how handy Facebook is for reconnecting with old friends. At 88, Betty said "if I want to connect with old friends, I need an Ouija board. Needless to say, when I was growing up we didn't have Facebook. We had a phone book, but you wouldn't waste an afternoon on it!"

She had some fun with some Facebook staples—such as the propensity of its users to post all their vacation photos, and for everyone to either list themselves as either "single" or in a relationship.

"When we were kids, we didn't say we were single," she said. "We were just kids. It was weird if you weren't single."[28]

Getting even more big laughs, she acknowledged that back in her day they did have "poking" (a greeting feature on Facebook), "but it wasn't something you did on a computer. It was something you did on a hayride, under a blanket."

The sketches were all built around Betty—including an opening segment set up as a frightening and awkward send up of *The Lawrence Welk Show*. Betty also made a bawdy appearance on a venerable *SNL* skit, a parody of a fictional NPR cooking show, "Delicious Dish," hosted by characters played by Anna Gasteyer and Molly Shannon.

While regular *SNL* fans may think Alec Baldwin "owns" the "Delicious Dish" skit for his earlier appearance as Pete Schweddy on the show to hawk his "Schweddy Christmas Balls"; Betty made the skit equally memorable.

Appearing as Florence Dusty, Betty's character is on "Delicious Dish" to tout her "Dusty Muffins"—an innuendo for an older woman's genitalia. Just as the writers had entirely too much fun working up sentences featuring the words "Schweddy Balls," the phrase "Dusty Muffin" had a hilarious set-up. "My muffins, I mean, I didn't know, or understand that that had anything wrong with it," Betty said, feigning innocence. "Just because I have a dusty muffin!"[29]

Later Betty did hilarious appearances as a hardened jail inmate in the regular "Scared Straight" segment with Keenan Thompson and as "MacGruber's" (Will Forte) grandmother in the regular parody of the old TV series, *MacGyver*. Seems all the *SNL* regulars wanted in on the act, as Betty also made appearances in favorite sketches including "Debby Downer" (with Rachel Dratch), "Licensed Joyologist" (with Molly Shannon), and as Andy Samberg's much older love interest on "Bronx Beat" (with Maya Rudolph and Amy Poehler).

Saturday Night Live was a throw-back to Betty's earliest days with live TV—but now she was almost 90 years old. The commercial breaks on the show are only 90 seconds, so the guest host is often yanked from one scene to the next to keep the show rolling along.

"They drag you into a dressing room closet about the size of a chair," Betty said, "and someone is doing your hair, and someone is doing your makeup, and someone is taking your clothes off, and someone else is putting them on. And then they drag you back on stage and you think, 'What sketch is this?'"[30]

ACADEMY AND OTHER HONORS

In April 2010, the American Academy of Television Arts and Sciences pulled out all the stops for its celebration of "Betty White: Celebrating 60 Years on Television." The star-studded event at Hollywood's Leonard H. Goldenson Theatre attracted many key starts from Betty's long career, including Mary Tyler Moore, Valerie Harper, Georgia Engel, Ed Asner, Cloris Leachman, Gavin MacLeod, Craig Ferguson, pianist Michael Feinstein, *Golden Girls* creator Susan Harris, cast members from CBS' daytime soap, *The Bold and the Beautiful*, and *Password* creator Bob Stewart.

Betty at the 61st Annual Primetime Creative Arts Emmy Awards at the Nokia Theatre in Los Angeles, September 2009. *(Shutterstock. com/S. Bukley)*

"White, herself resplendent in cream and gold, received a standing ovation when she entered," wrote the Academy's Libby Slate about the memorable evening. "I can't believe the people who showed up!" a clearly excited Betty told the audience.[31]

Awards were nothing new for Betty—she was a frequently honored star. In 1976, she won the "Golden Ike Award" from Pacific Pioneers in Broadcasting, and the Genii Award from the Association of American Women in Radio and TV. American Comedy Awards also came her way in 1987 as "Funniest Female," and again in 1990 as a Lifetime Achievement Winner.

In January 2010, Betty received the esteemed "Lifetime Achievement Award" from the Screen Actors' Guild. "Whether creating some of television's most indelible characters, plunging into film roles with joyous gusto or perfecting the art of the quip as a television panelist and host, Betty White has entertained audiences with her impeccable comic timing and remarkable wit for more than 60 years," said Alan Rosenberg, national president of the Screen Actors' Guild.[32]

The Television Academy's Hall of Fame inducted Betty in 1995. Betty was the only woman included in the 11th class of inductees to the Hall of Fame. Other members of her class were Michael Landon, Richard Levinson, William Link, Jim McKay, Bill Moyers, and Dick Van Dyke.

Betty joins *Glee* star Jane Lynch on the red carpet at the 19th Annual British Academy of Film and Television Arts—or BAFTA Awards—in November 2010 in Century City, CA. *(Shutterstock.com/Helga Esteb)*

TV Land, the cable network built off the power of reruns, began its own "TV Land Awards" and in 2008 honored the cast of *The Golden Girls* with its "Pop Culture Award."

The TV Land Awards ended up being important and revealing. Important because it was the last time three of the Golden Girls were together in public. Revealing because of the event's "red carpet" video of Betty and co-stars Rue McClanahan and Bea Arthur displayed the somewhat declining health of Arthur. Arthur seemed reluctant to step out front for photos with the paparazzi, instead holding tight to McClanahan's arm the whole time.

Later on stage, Arthur seemed at a loss for a funny line, but saved the moment by saying, "Rue is the funny one—at least *she* thinks so."

McClanahan said the TV Land Award resembled her third husband, while Betty declared the best part of the award for her was the fact that it brought the three of them together. No on-camera mention was made of fellow co-star Estelle Getty (who made her last public appearance eight years earlier in 2000).

The following year, in 2009, Betty was honored with the Lifetime Achievement Award from the Television Critics' Association.

And we haven't even mentioned TV's highest honor—the Emmy award—that Betty has practically owned across six decades. Two of those Emmys were for the Sue Ann Nivens character on *The Mary Tyler Moore Show*—a lucky strike after a long dry spell. "Talk about a thrill," she said. "I went 22 years between my first Emmy and the next one. When they announced my name that night, oh that was incredible. And it was Ed Asner who was presenting the award to me. I was a mess. I was so excited, and so happy, and so grateful for the opportunity."[33]

The awards turned her career around, Betty believes, even though it took many years of toiling on game shows and with guest spots on other established shows. Grateful for all the TV appearances along the way, Betty noted that game and talk show appearances are "not the same as being an actor, there is a difference, and so everybody was so surprised that Betty could act."[34]

Betty believes TV has given her a lot and she believes in giving back. In June 2012 she led a ribbon-cutting for the Chicago Museum of Broadcast Communications. "Television is my life, and it's been very good to me," she said. "I'm still in the business. My health and energy are good and I'm being invited to keep working. That makes me very happy."[35]

In 2012, Betty was nominated for more Emmy awards—this time for *Betty White's Off Their Rockers*—an NBC show she described as "a hidden camera show but this time its old people putting young people on. They allow young 'turks' to hear some pretty outrageous stuff, all staged, of course. I think the results are pretty funny."[36]

Interestingly, although Betty was not nominated individually, NBC's gala birthday celebration for Betty White that aired in January 2012, won Emmy nominations as well. The show was a big ratings hit for the ratings-challenged Peacock network as has been Betty's reality show. In May, *Betty White's Off Their Rockers* scored an unusual accomplishment—attracting more than 5 million viewers in the 18-49 year-old audience, a higher share than Fox's mega-hit *American Idol*, ABC's *The Middle*, or CBS' *Survivor* in the same timeslot.[37]

Critics were surprised by Betty's latest Emmy nomination for her *Off Their Rockers* show—some of them noting that it was mostly a courtesy. But her nomination did succeed in pushing Jeff Probst out of the category. Probst has won multiple Emmys in his role as host of CBS' mega-hit reality series, *Survivor*. As *The Washington Post* put it, if Betty had won the Emmy, "it would be something new for the category, though scarcely what you'd call progress."[38]

Betty tapes her NBC reality show, *Off Their Rockers*, and the TV Land sitcom *Hot in Cleveland* at the same time—"which is going to take a little pre-planning and stuff, but we'll get it done. I'll be glad to be getting back to work. When you love what you do, it's not work. I'm privileged at 90 years old to still be invited to do this stuff. They haven't been able to get rid of me."[39]

2
_____

White Hot

Still Hot in Cleveland

A prime example of Betty's staying power is written all over her hit cable series, *Hot In Cleveland*. The show premiered to 4.75 million viewers in its first week and was the most watched show ever for TV Land. After just four episodes, the cable network announced it had picked up the show for a full season of 10 episodes—and three more full seasons have followed.[40]

The fast start for *Hot In Cleveland* and the more than respectable showing on *SNL* was no big surprise—Betty was ubiquitous in promoting the shows, most especially the TV Land effort that brought her together with three other established primetime female stars—Valerie Bertinelli (from CBS' *One Day At A Time*), Jane Leeves (from NBC's *Frasier*), and Wendie Malick (from NBC's *Just Shoot Me*).

Her presence on *Hot in Cleveland*, however, was supposed to be a one-time, "guest shot" for the series pilot only. Series creator Suzanne Martin and her co-executive producers, Lynda

The cast of TV Land's *Hot in Cleveland* in the green room back stage at the April 2011 gala, "Actors and Others for Animals," at the Universal Hilton Hotel in Los Angeles. From left are co-stars Wendie Malick, Betty, Jane Leeves, and Valerie Bertinelli. *(Shutterstock.com/Helga Esteb)*

Obst, Sean Hayes (Jack from NBC's mega-hit *Will & Grace*), and Todd Milliner, had other ideas.

"Quite seriously, when (the show) got picked up so quickly, I was thrilled for these ladies (Valerie, Jane and Wendie)," Betty said. "They got picked up for 10 episodes and then they came to me and said, 'Will you do a few more?' I said, 'I'm sorry, I can't' and then they started the 'what ifs' with me—and I wasn't trying to be coy."[41]

Betty's schedule was full and her every instinct told her to tell the TV Land folks thanks, but no thanks. But a good time taping the show's pilot, use of the traditional four-camera set-up for a sitcom, and the enjoyment of taping the show in front of a live (and in this case, loud and enthusiastic) audience at CBS' Studio City, sealed the deal.

Adding some sugar to the deal, Betty's excitement with *Hot in Cleveland* meant she would once again be part of a TV show that broke barriers. Just as *The Golden Girls* had blasted through tradition and brought—gasp—women over the age of 40 back to TV, *Hot in Cleveland* was doing the same.

"I have the backbone of a jelly fish, so I gave in," Betty said. "Then we got picked up for 20 episodes, and guess who did all 20?! I guess they can't drive me away."[42]

Betty's character, Elka Ostrovsky, was originally cast as the grouchy and highly territorial caretaker for an old barn of a house in Cleveland that Melanie, Joy, and Victoria (played, respectively, by Bertinelli, Leeves and Malick) decide to rent. The premise of the show reveals the three younger women are refugees from L.A. held over from a flight in Cleveland. They grow disgusted at how their age renders them virtually invisible to men in California; they find they are indeed "hot" in Cleveland—where the standards are different.

Elka—who has mellowed a bit over the three seasons (with perhaps an exception of regularly airing bitterness toward Leeves' character), has a bit of a mysterious past. References to escaping the Nazis during World War II and a basement filled with stolen goods and marijuana from her mob-connected "dead" husband— Betty has a lot to work with in creating Elka.

Betty admits she's working hard to contrast Elka with the personas so well known to TV audiences through her memorable characters, Sue Ann Nivens and Rose Nylund.

"Because Elka is a smart-ass character, I am trying to keep her away from those other two ladies (Sue Ann and Rose) that I love very much," Betty said. "I have such an opportunity, and as the show has evolved, Elka started out as a heavy; she was a villain."

Elka truly does love the other girls renting the house—though they are about half her age—"and we're really a foursome, we're really a group that can stand up against the world and support each other."[43]

Sound familiar? It's a winning combination—"four perfect points on a compass," Betty calls it—that worked so well for so long on *The Golden Girls*.

Hot in Cleveland also breaks a lot of traditional primetime TV rules when it comes to casting. Because the show is on TV Land, a cable network that exists for the sole purpose of celebrating classic TV shows, there is no shortage of classic stars that have made their way through Cleveland. The guest list so far includes—Ed Asner, Tim Bagley, Orson Bean, Sandra Bernhard, Barry Bostwick, Cedric the Entertainer, Kristen Chenowith, Tim Conway, Dan Cortese, Georgia Engle, Dave Foley, Bonnie Franklin, Willie Garson, Laura San Giacomo, Kathie Lee Gifford, Melanie Griffith, Gregory Harrison, Sean Hayes, Jennifer Love Hewitt, Buck Henry, Mark Indelicato, Joe Jonas, Shirley Jones, Wayne Knight, Steve Lawrence, Huey Lewis, Hal Linden, Jon Lovitz, Susan Lucci, John Mahoney, Gilles Marini, Wendi McLendon-Covey, Juliet Mills, Mary Tyler Moore, Isaiah Mustafa, Kevin Nealon, Rhea Perlman, Regis Philbin, Carl Reiner, Andy Richter, Don Rickles, Joan Rivers, Doris Roberts, Antonio Sabato, Jr., Cybill Shepherd, Jonathan Silverman, John Schneider, Amy Sedaris, David Spade, Rick Springfield, and Steven Weber.

Hot in Cleveland gives Betty many golden moments to shine against the younger cast—noting from her "bedazzled" sweat suit that "When you're 20, you dress for love; when you're 40, you dress for success; and when you're 80, you dress for the bathroom!"[44]

Further, since her character Elka is apparently still sexually active and dating, a strong storyline involving guest stars Carl Reiner and Tim Conway yielded tons of laughs—including a truly risqué discussion of why Elka wanted to break up with Reiner's character—"he doesn't like to go downtown." Turns out, Reiner's character doesn't like driving in heavy downtown traffic, but the audience's dirty mind produced a lot of laughs.

Many episodes of *Hot* have Betty's character Elka front and center, including:

 SEASON ONE

Pilot Episode—Originally broadcast June 16, 2010
Betty stole the show as the grumpy and territorial caretaker of the Cleveland house that Melanie, Victoria and Joy decide to rent. Joy gets off on the wrong foot with Elka asking her about the smell of marijuana emanating from the basement. Elka replies, "What business is it of yours? Are you a cop?"

It's Not That Complicated—Originally broadcast July 28, 2010
Elka is at the center of a love triangle with guest stars Carl Reiner and Tim Conway desperately competing for her affections.

Good Luck with Faking the Goiter—Originally broadcast August 11, 2010
Victoria is looking for some positive publicity, so she agrees to Elka's scheme to fake a debilitating disease, allowing her to demonstrate how strong she is. Trouble is, Elka has cooked up a horrible disease with dozens of horrible symptoms, including a large, football-sized neck goiter!

Tornado!—Originally broadcast August 18, 2010
As a tornado rips through Ohio the girls flee to the basement only to discover Elka's secret stash of stolen goods left by her dearly departed, yet mob-connected husband. Elka's in trouble as Melanie's new boyfriend, a Cleveland police officer, is obligated to arrest and lock-up the elderly and uncooperative Elka in the Season 1 finale.

 SEASON TWO

Free Elka—Originally broadcast January 19, 2011
The second season gets off to an incredibly funny start as Elka is locked up on various charges and finds herself cell mates with none other than guest star Mary Tyler Moore. Mary plays a hard-edged jailhouse veteran as the girls try to raise bail money to get Elka out.

Hot for Lawyer—Originally broadcast February 2, 2011
Elka's attorney is using an unusual approach to try and get her out from under criminal charges—claim Elka is mentally incompetent due to her age. Elka plays along—as do Victoria and Joy who find her young attorney irresistible. Elka foils all the plans, however, when her true competency shines through as she learns her true love (frequent guest star Carl Reiner) is getting married to someone else.

Elka's Snowbird—Originally broadcast March 16, 2011
Carl Reiner is back again as Elka's love interest Max. Elka succeeded in keeping Max from marrying someone else, but now Max wants to move to Florida to avoid the winter winds of Cleveland.

Law and Elka—Originally broadcast March 23, 2011
Elka's criminal trial is finally at hand—the incompetency effort a complete failure. A new approach is cooked up, this time Elka seduces the oldest juror in the room—or perhaps in the world. Elka's convinced her scheme has won her acquittal, only to learn the old man juror suffers frequent memory loss, and can't remember having had a good time with Elka! As is possible with cable TV series, the producers leave viewers wondering Elka's fate in the requisite TV cliffhanger. When the subsequent episode, *Where's Elka?* (broadcast June 15, 2011) finally airs, Elka has disappeared deep into Amish country in rural Ohio.

Dancing Queens—Originally broadcast July 20, 2011
Melanie, Victoria and Joy decide they need to be BFFs with gay men. They decide to visit a local gay bar to try and meet new friends, and Elka tags along. Turns out guest star Doris Roberts (one of Elka's old rivals) owns the bar.

Indecent Proposals—Originally broadcast August 17, 2011
Victoria is doing a local news feature story about whether men and women can be friends with no sexual contact between them. The show's premise gives producers another chance to dig up one of Elka's old flames, with guest star Buck Henry appearing as Fred.

Bridezelka—Originally broadcast August 24, 2011
Elka and Fred are hitting it off so well that a quick wedding
is planned, with none other than Cedric the Entertainer
standing in as the minister. Elka's original plans for a simple
wedding go by the wayside as the girls encourage her to have
a big blast—unknowingly, however, unleashing a "Bridezilla"
in the form of Elka.

Elka's Wedding—Originally broadcast August 31, 2011
Season two comes to a finale with Elka's wedding day at
hand—but Elka is missing. Not surprising—the bachelorette
party the night before finds the house filled with hung-
over drunk college guys, and an iguana on the loose. The
cliffhanger centers on the girls desperately seeking Elka in
time for the wedding.

 **SEASON THREE**

Elka's Choice—Originally broadcast November 30, 2011
The third season kicks off with another surprise. Getting Elka
married off to her new love Fred (guest star Buck Henry) hits
a major roadblock when not only does former flame Max
(guest star Carl Reiner) shows up to complicate things, but so
does Elka's presumably "dead" husband, Bobby (guest star
Don Rickles). The three men compete for Elka's affections
with hilarious results.

Funeral Crashers—Originally broadcast December 14, 2011
Elka comes to the rescue to try and recover Melanie's
favorite dress that the dry cleaner has given to another
customer—a corpse at the local funeral home! Yet another
suitor for Elka's affections arrives—guest star John Mahoney
playing the younger man—Roy.

God and Football—Originally broadcast January 18, 2012
The show's producers don't shy away from Betty's real age—
as the girls celebrate Elka's 90th birthday as well. Melanie's
plan, however, to surprise Elka with a visit with her beloved
Cleveland Browns goes awry—in the locker-room! Victoria's
near-death experience also brings her face-to-face with

who she thinks is God—Elka. Elka ends up telling Victoria, repeatedly, to "walk away from the light!"

Rubber Ball—Originally broadcast March 21, 2012
The girls want to join a prestigious Cleveland country club, and of course, Elka has a past there too! A former waitress at the club, as a young woman Elka was fired by her lecherous boss (guest star Ed Asner). Elka vows revenge on Asner's character by fooling him to fall in love with her, as Joy has some hilarious moments with another guest star, Jon Lovitz. Elka's chasing of Asner is nothing new—Betty's character Sue Ann Nivens was known to have strongly amorous feelings for Asner's Lou Grant character a few decades ago!

Hot and Heavy—Originally broadcast March 14, 2012
Elka pushes her way into Victoria's plans to go undercover at an Overeaters' Anonymous meeting. Elka ridiculously claims to have lost 600 pounds—and confesses to her low point of obesity—eating a ham she found hidden in the folds of her back fat!

Bye George, I Think He's Got It!—Originally broadcast April 25, 2012
Guest star Joan Rivers shows up as Elka's long-lost twin sister. Forget the fact that Betty and Joan look nothing alike, with a guest star like the latter, it's all played for big laughs.

For someone who was supposed to be a guest star only in the pilot episode, the writers and producers of *Hot in Cleveland* have run with a good thing and promoted Betty's character Elka to the center of the action. It's not that Betty minds. She says, "It's such a delightful show to do because again, the chemistry between those girls is so wonderful that you get the feeling that something good is happening."[45]

Beyond perfect casting, Betty loves the fact the show is taped live in front of a studio audience. "It's such a joy," she said. "It's like live theatre. You go in and you've got your studio audience like we have here, and they help you, they tell you when you have to pause for a laugh, and wait for your next line, or when you put a pause in and there is no laugh, you learn to move right along!"[46]

On Cable—Going a Little Blue

On Comedy Central's wildly popular *Daily Show with Jon Stewart*, Betty sparred suitably with the sardonic Stewart who asked her, "Are there any people in your life who can still say no to Betty White?" Betty's reply was classic: "I haven't found any."[47]

Stewart also took the occasion of the meeting to warn Betty against going into "a Britney Phase," a reference to the over-exposure problems experienced by pop star icon Britney Spears.

Betty also reminded audiences that "I won't do drug jokes. Every once in a while someone will write something (in a script) and say it would be funny if all the old ladies smoked pot or something . . . (but) I just don't think drugs are funny, and I don't like to make jokes about them."[48]

Not surprisingly, any jokes at the expense of animals were also off limits, Betty told Stewart.[49]

Some of the magic of Betty's comedy has always been the suggestive, or just under the surface, naughtiness of her jokes. The double entendre, which she perfected, relies completely on that premise. "Just under the surface" is not a phrase shock comedienne Kathy Griffin is too familiar with—as evidenced by her successful, yet often bawdy Bravo cable network franchise, *Kathy Griffin: My Life on the 'D List.'*

Betty appeared on the show in 2009 by meeting up with Kathy and her 80-something mom for lunch at—of all places—the Sizzler. While cozying up to the salad bar, Kathy led the girls in an R-rated version of *Password*. Betty was apparently a willing participant, the segment ending with the eyebrow raising and "beeped" retort from Betty: "Kathy, bless her heart, can bastardize just about anything with her naughty words. And I rise above that (beep)."[50]

The "blue" comedy continued when the New York Friar's Club "roasted" Betty at New York's famed Globe Theatre. As Barbara

Walters told the audience, "Betty is not the first woman to be roasted by the Friars, but there have been so many firsts for her. Betty was the first woman to do Shakespeare at the Globe Theatre. I mean literally. She did him in the balcony!"[51]

At the roast, Betty arrived on stage on a white pony accompanied by two shirtless muscle men in their 20s. Larry King made the trip from L.A. to New York to roast Betty noting, "What's going to bother Betty White? When you're over 90, what, are you going to ruin her career?" King added that at Betty's age "there is a fine line between a roast and a cremation. Betty is so old, she remembers the first days of Pompeii. She's so old, she thinks I'm jail bait."[52]

Jokes about King and Betty also made the list—with *Hot in Cleveland* co-star Jane Leeves noting, "Betty is so old, she babysat Larry King!"

Sharp-tongued co-host of ABC's *The View*, Joy Behar was there and added, "Betty is so old, her first sitcom was called *Hot for Grover Cleveland*."

Comedian Jeffrey Ross noted that the roast for Betty was scheduled as a luncheon rather than a dinner, for fear that Betty couldn't stay up late enough for dinner. After all, he said, "Betty is the only person here who truly saw *The Titanic* in 3-D." Fellow comedian Lisa Lampanelli added, "Betty White is so old that on her first game show, the grand prize was fire."[53]

Other roasters included Katie Couric, Matt Lauer, Liza Minnelli, Dick Cavett, Susan Lucci, Valerie Harper, Regis Philbin, Valerie Bertinelli, and Abe Vigoda.

Betty's Birthday Suit?

Betty's meteoric rise in popularity in the first decade of the 21st century was not without some controversy. Old problems surfaced now and again—stories alleging a cache of nude photos of Betty and her late husband found stashed in one of her former houses, and claims that she remained estranged from one of her stepdaughters.

"This is simply not her," Betty's agent Jeff Witjas informed ABCNews.com about renewed claims that the buyer of White's former Los Angeles home found the photos. "This has come up over the years, people claim they have photos of Betty and Allen (Ludden), and it's simply not true. And Betty's laughing. She can't believe people are still talking about this."[54]

Witjas said he had batted down the nude Betty rumors before—but it was Betty herself who more than suggested at least one photo of her was in fact, her. During a 1985 appearance on NBC's *Late Night with David Letterman*, White was shown a nine of hearts playing card showing a topless White wearing only earmuffs. White's response? A quick denial, followed by a cryptic statement: "It does look like me except the ear muffs would not have been there, they would have been here," pointing at her breasts.[55]

White admits she has a "bawdy" sense of humor. "I have to keep my mental editor awake at times," she said on ABC's *Nightline*. "But I love the double entendre. If somebody gets it, they laugh and think it's funny, and if they don't get it, who knows—and it doesn't matter."[56]

Her love of the double entendre was in full swing when CNN's Entertainment Blog editor asked her if after six decades, there was "anything Betty White still wants to do?"

Without missing a beat, Betty offers, "My answer to every question is Robert Redford, but I've never met him and I don't want to meet him. I've taken his name in vain so many times I'd be embarrassed if I met him."[57]

The idea of meeting Redford is one that worries Betty—she's afraid that her jokes at his expense would make a meeting uncomfortable. "I have taken that poor man's name in vain so many times, I'm really getting paranoid about it," she said. "He is a very shy, caring, outgoing person."[58]

Redford is also a gentleman, Betty reports. In the days after she received a Lifetime Achievement Award from the Screen Actors Guild, a letter arrived from Redford that included a six-stanza poem. "I won't tell you what the last two lines of the poem were, but they were pretty funny," Betty said.[59]

Betty's love of Redford, she said, is not "just another movie star crush" but is more based on Redford's commitment to the environment and other shared political interests. "He has done so much for the film industry too," Betty said. "Those are the things that I fell in love with. Just the fact that I talk about him, I'm just trying to move myself up in class."[60]

Betty is not immune from controversy, even as a senior citizen. In 2012, a television watchdog group known as the Parents Television Council issued its list of 76 instances of nudity in primetime TV. Of the 37 shows the conservative group said "went there" with nudity, NBC's new hit *Betty White's Off Their Rockers* was cited even though the nudity was, the group acknowledged, only "suggested" via pixilated on-screen images. The Parents Television Council forwarded its concerns to the Federal Communications Commission, but no action was taken by the FCC as even the sexy references contained in Betty's new show were done within television's strict appropriateness guidelines.[61]

Betty on the Big Screen

Officially, Betty has appeared in about two dozen major motion pictures, but beyond *Time to Kill* in 1945 and *Advice and Consent* 17 years later in 1962, all of Betty's film roles have come late in her career.

Time to Kill was released just as World War II was coming to an end and starred George Reeves, DeForest Kelley, and Jimmy Lydon as a group of sailors. Betty played the bright-eyed, loyal love interest for Lydon's character "Lou."

Time to Kill was a short, 23-minute film produced by the First Motion Picture Unit of the U.S. Army Air Forces. Betty was just 23 years old when it was filmed. Hardly a Hollywood epic, the film focused on the male characters as they played cards and teased their shipmate "Frank" played by Reeves, about constantly reading. But all that reading was for a reason, the sailors would soon learn, as Frank is studying to get a high school diploma so he can qualify for all of the educational benefits offered by the Armed Forces Institute. The other fellows soon realize their life dreams can come true through a commitment to learning, and to the armed services. The film fit its war-time era—it was pure Army propaganda.

Her second film, 1962's *Advice and Consent* paired Betty alongside an all-star cast under the direction of famed director Otto Preminger. While Betty's name did not make the movie poster, it's rather understandable given the sparkling line-up of bigger names in the cast, including Henry Fonda, Charles Laughton, Don Murray, Walter Pidgeon, Peter Lawford, Gene Tierney, and Burgess Meredith. Betty's character was "Senator Bessie Adams" of Kansas—and was not central to the storyline based on Allen Drury's best-selling 1959 novel that canvasses the presidential nomination of a new Secretary of State, and the dramatic political back and forth that resulted.

The film was generally panned by critics—with reviewers from *Variety* and *The New York Times* praising the acting, but panning the storyline and directing. The film was controversial for its time for its open suggestion of a homosexual relationship between two of the male characters, and harbingers back to the "Red scare" era of Hollywood that found Washington power-brokers questioning the loyalty and backgrounds of most every motion picture star.

In 1998 Betty was cast in the disaster-thriller film, *Hard Rain* that featured Christian Slater, Morgan Freeman, Randy Quaid, Minnie Driver, and Betty's old co-MTM co-star, Edward Asner. The film centered on a heist in the midst of a natural disaster in a small Indiana town. The film's tagline summed up the simple plot, "A simple plan. An instant fortune. Just add water." Betty's character Doreen Sears played opposite character actor Richard Dysart and was one of the local Indiana townsfolk on the sidelines of the main story.

That same year she appeared in the family-oriented *Dennis the Menace Strikes Again* from Warner Brothers. Betty's character, Martha, helps Dennis (played by child actor Justin Cooper) get started on his pranks. Also appearing were Don Rickles, George Kennedy, Brian Doyle-Murray and "Carrot Top" (AKA Scott Thompson).

More readily forgotten is her cameo appearance in Eddie Murphy's major flop, *Holy Man* from '98 that also starred Jeff Goldblum and Kelly Preston. Betty's role is credited only as a "cameo"—which is a good thing. The film was a major box office and critical disaster.

Certainly more memorable (and meaningful for Betty's career) was her 1999 appearance in David E. Kelley's dark film, *Lake Placid*. Betty plays Delores Bickerman, a lakeside resident suspected of having killed her husband. The film attempts to tell the tale of two, 30-foot man-eating crocodiles that terrorize the small Maine town near the lake—beasts that Betty's character has apparently fed not only her husband, but other food as well. Playing way-against-type, when the local sheriff asks Betty's character whether she killed her husband, she replies bluntly: "If I had a dick, this is where I would tell you to suck it."

Although not a box office hit—and panned by some critics—
Lake Placid developed the cult following that seems to attach to
any Kelley efforts (and prompted two made-for-TV sequels).

Later that year Betty joined TV-actor-turned-successful-
director Rob Reiner in his Castle Rock Entertainment production,
The Story of Us starring Bruce Willis and Michele Pfeiffer. Betty
played Lillian Jordan in the film that traces a married couple over
a 15-year-period and their attempts to weather, and ultimately
rise above, the challenges and difficulties that would seemingly
pull them apart.

Less notable parts followed in the subsequent years, including
a voice role in the animated features *Whispers: An Elephant's Tale*
and *Tom Sawyer* and the live-action, dog-centered comedy *The
Retrievers*. In 2005, Betty also appeared in the successful made-
for-TV movie, *Annie's Point*.

Screen success would return in 2009, in part because of
Betty's ability to steal the show. *The Proposal* starred Hollywood
mega-stars Sandra Bullock and Ryan Reynolds. Betty helped fill
out a supporting cast that also included established actors Mary
Steenburgen, Craig T. Nelson, and Oscar Nunez.

The film tells the story of domineering female boss Margaret
Tate, played by Bullock, who rules over her personal assistant
Andrew, played by Reynolds. If Bullock's profit-driven character
wants to remain in the U.S. (since she's Canadian and her work
visa is about to expire), she must enlist Reynolds' character for
a shotgun wedding. Betty plays "Gammy," or unexpectedly hip
Grandma Annie in Andrew's Alaskan family. Most fans can recite
word-for-word Betty's scene-stealing performances, including
trying to fit Bullock for the family heirloom wedding dress and
referring to her bosom as "Easter eggs."

Promoting *The Proposal* seemed to bring out the best in
Betty—as evidenced by a lively appearance on the *CBS Morning*

Show. Host Harry Smith asked Betty the classic question, "Is there anything left that you would still like to do in show business?"

With her classic timing, Betty replied: "Robert Redford."

She wasn't done. Smith asked, "After more than 60 years in show business, do you still pinch yourself and say, 'How lucky am I?'"

Betty shot back: "Boy, do I ever! And I even have people in to pinch me sometimes."

Noting that the CBS show was broadcasting live from aboard a U.S. Naval aircraft carrier, Smith asked Betty if she ever had a chance to entertain the troops.

"On my own time? Every chance I got," she said.

The Proposal was panned by critics for its lightweight fare—but fans loved it—making it the No. 1 romantic comedy released in 2009. It grossed $317 million for its producers back at Touchstone Pictures—pretty impressive for a film that cost *only* $40 million to make. The film also won a variety of awards from shows as diverse as the *People's Choice Award, the MTV Movie Awards, the Kid's Choice Awards, the Teen Choice Awards*, and *The Golden Globes* (the latter of which awarded Bullock its Best Actress Award for a musical or comedy). Betty took home the "Best WTF Moment Award"—whatever that is—from the MTV confab.

In 2009 Betty also lent her voice to the animated feature, *Ponyo*, that won most of its followers in Japan. In 2010 she also appeared as Grandma Bunny in the comedy romp, *You Again*, from Touchstone Pictures.

In June 2010, the Screen Actors Guild tapped Bullock to introduce Betty's "Lifetime Achievement Award." The well-liked Hollywood starlet proved up to the task, in deadpan telling the audience, "I know that a lot of people find Betty White inspiring. Me, I find Betty White annoying. I'm sorry. It's true." [62]

Betty was front and center for the September 2010 Los Angeles premiere of *You Again?*, a Touchstone Pictures release that starred (from left) Sigourney Weaver, Odette Yustman, Betty, Kristen Bell, and Jamie Lee Curtis. *(Shutterstock.com/Helga Esteb)*

Betty was ready in waiting—when it came her turn, she motioned to Bullock and told the audience: "She is such a wonderful one. With all the wonderful things that have happened to her, isn't it heartening to see how far a girl as plain as she is can go?"[63]

Betty said she was excited to receive the honor from SAG—but told comedian George Lopez on his late-night TBS show, *Lopez Tonight*, that at her age, "I just wish they wouldn't call it the 'sag' award."[64]

In 2012, Betty actively promoted the film, *Dr. Seuss' The Lorax*—a film she was drawn to because of the environmental components to the story. Based on Seuss' 1971 children's classic,

Betty played Grammy Norma in a production that starred Zac Efron, Danny DeVito, and Taylor Swift. "I think it's a beautiful story," Betty said. "The whole production is beautiful so I was delighted to be brought into it."[65]

Betty admits, however, that she sees herself as a little like the character Grammy Norma. "I think of myself more like, you know, the glamour girl," she deadpans. "A gorgeous, gorgeous person and somehow I don't think that equates with how other people see me."[66]

3

Life with Betty

Betty's Early Life

That Betty would enjoy success late in her life on the silver screen was something that she thought little of in her early life, though she grew up in the shadows of the major Hollywood studios. In those days, the film industry must have seemed a million miles away, though it was just a short car ride away from her childhood home in Los Angeles.

The White family originally lived at 454 Harper Avenue in L.A., just a few blocks south of Melrose Avenue, and closer to West Hollywood than Beverly Hills. The Spanish-style house was built in 1928, and the White's lived there until Betty's school years when they moved to Beverly Hills (where she attended Horace Mann School).

Betty's early life as an only child was as wonderful as anyone who grew up with lots of brothers and sisters can imagine. Family pets and neighborhood pals filled in where siblings would have been—and Betty grew up accustomed to being the center of attention.

Always the animal lover, here's Betty at home in October 1954 with her St. Bernard Stormy. *(Bettmann/Corbiss/ AP Images)*

A childhood highlight Betty liked to remember were summer trips for the family into the California High Sierras for three weeks at a time.

"We would ride in and the camping equipment would be on the mule pack," Betty said. "They would leave us there and come back in three weeks. Christmas was nice, but I used to live all year for those High Sierra trips."[67]

It was in childhood that Betty fell in love with animals—most especially dogs. It was a love her father imparted to her.

"As extra work, Dad would make radios to sell and make some extra money," she said. "No one else had any money either. He'd trade them for animals. Well, radios don't eat, but animals do, so it wasn't the best business deal he ever made."[68]

Amazingly, Betty was a Hollywood kid almost from the start—but it didn't seem to show. Born in Oak Park, Illinois, by age two the White family had moved to California. "I was not really aware of the studios until she wrote a school play," she said where she promptly wrote herself into the lead role.

Betty also briefly took opera training as a girl—"I would have been an opera singer, although I lacked one major thing, a talent for that."[69]

Betty attended Beverly Hills High School—a school that has produced a variety of other stars from yesterday and today—including Corbin Bernsen, Albert Brooks, Nicholas Cage, Jackie Cooper, Rhonda Fleming, Crispin Glover, Lenny Kravitz, Rob Reiner, David Schwimmer, and Antonio Sobato, Jr.

For her 1939 graduation from Beverly Hills High, Betty was tapped to sing at the Commencement exercises—choosing a serious song called "Spirit Flower." Her graduation gown would come in handy for her next "stage" performance.

A True TV Pioneer

Just after high school, Betty put on her graduation gown again and joined Class President Harry Bennett to participate in an unusual experiment—what Betty considered "science fiction."

A group of inventors had created one of the very earliest versions of TV transmission. She and Bennett were asked to portray a segment of "The Mary Widow" in front of cameras on the sixth floor of the Packard auto dealership building in downtown Los Angeles. The inventors had rigged up a monitor in the Packard showroom that "broadcast" the play segment being acted out live six floors above the showroom.

"That was my debut in television, but I really didn't go to work in it until 1949," she said.[70]

World War II had intervened between Betty's graduation and the start-up years for television. Betty and her mom Tess joined the American Women's Voluntary Services, and served coffee at events for soldiers and sailors, and also went with her mom to do alterations and sewing.

The acting bug was still bighting her—however—and she got a job at a local theatre by *paying the theatre $50 a month tuition.* "You could read for the plays or be on the stage crew," she said.

Eventually she won a lead role and the theatre *paid her* $50. After that, Betty got wise. "I'd go around to radio stations on Tuesdays, which were casting days—and hung around as much as she could. Eventually someone would think you looked familiar and would cast you in a show, thinking they had used you before. My parts were limited to making background sounds such as 'Hello!' or 'Merry Christmas!'" Betty said.[71]

To get serious about acting, though, she'd have to join the union, but had to have a paid acting credit under her name to get in. "It cost $67 to get into the union—[and I got an acting] job that paid $37—so I borrowed the rest from my father. He was pretty excited, and he said 'If you don't get to work too often, you might make some money," she said.[72]

Betty soon found a home at KLAC Radio—one of the first and most powerful radio stations in Los Angeles and southern California. Asked if she could sing, she soon joined Dick Haines, a popular DJ at the time, and was offered a role on his show that did not pay—singing two songs. "Slow Boat to China" and "Somebody Loves You."

Not surprisingly, KLAC Radio was soon to become—KLAC-TV— reflecting the arrival of a new, modern medium: Television. KLAC put together its own line-up of programs, including a quiz and panel show called *Grab Your Phone.* Betty started as one of four girls answering the phones for listeners calling in with answers—a job that paid $10 a week.

Another KLAC personality, Al Jarvis, was hosting his own show (*The Al Jarvis Talent Show*) and saw Betty on *Grab Your Phone* and called her up—and asked her to be his "Girl Friday" on his TV show. Jarvis' job paid $50 a week—but the show started out rather weakly as Jarvis just tried to bring his radio show to TV, playing records and talking and visiting in between the songs.

"While the records were on, the TV audience could see him— and they scrubbed the records part of it," Betty said.[73]

Out of necessity to show something more interesting than two people waiting for a phonograph record to end, the TV talk show was born with Jarvis and Betty ad-libbing live each day for five hours. Soon they were on six days a week. One of only two TV stations on the air in L.A. at the time, Jarvis and Betty were on air for about 33 hours a week. Her salary eventually grew to $300 a week.

"I know people make millions of dollars now, but that $300 a week meant the world to me, I thought I had really made it," she said.[74]

The show was truly live—no tapes of any kind existed at that point. Even the advertisements were live—Betty recalled doing as many as 54 ads in one show—all of them ad-libbed from typed copy on note cards handed to her from production staff. There were no rehearsals either.

"It was like going to Television College because I was there for four years, and I learned it all," she said.[75]

Actor Eddie Albert eventually joined the show replacing Jarvis, but didn't stay long and KLAC executives gave Betty a break and made her the center of the show, now going by the name *Hollywood on Television*.

It was hard work—and held no promise of anything further to come. Regardless, Betty valued every moment of it. From it she gained advice she offered young actors she met: "Take any job that comes your way, and do it to the best of your ability. What's happened to the business nowadays, a lot of the young people have gotten into a series and become big stars overnight, major stars. They make a lot of money and they are absolutely incredible. Now, when that show ends they think they just pick up on the next thing, and it doesn't work like that. You've got to pay your dues."[76]

Betty's First Two Marriages

Betty's commitment to a career in TV and entertainment may have produced perhaps the greatest regret of her life: two failed marriages—both ones that barely lasted beyond the honeymoon. In 1945, Betty married and divorced Dick Barker, identified as a chicken farmer and World War II fighter pilot.

"Within weeks of V-E Day, I married Dick, a P-38 pilot . . . and he told me after we had been married that he had been mustered out (of the Air Force)," she said.[77]

The young couple left California for Barker's hometown of Belle Center, Ohio—a tiny town tucked away in the Ohio farm country outside Lima, Ohio. "There were just 800 people there, and that was a real adjustment," Betty, the Los Angeles-raised girl said. "We finally moved back (to L.A.), but that one didn't work out."[78]

Divorced after such a brief marriage, Betty moved back home with her parents.

"You feel like a real failure," she said. "After Dick and I broke up, I went to a little theatre in Beverly Hills and was doing some shows there."[79]

It was there in 1946-47 she met her next husband, another World War II veteran—Lane Allen—a man differing from Barker by the fact that he wanted to stay in Hollywood and work as a casting agent.

"He asked me out after one of the shows, and he was a delightful man, a lovely man," she said. "We fell very much in love."[80]

The young couple married in 1949 just as Betty was being cast as a sidekick on a new Los Angeles-based TV show, *Hollywood on Television*. It was a career choice that was soon to conflict with the couple's personal life.

"We met through my career, but we had a major problem once it was underway," she said. "He just couldn't stand me spending that kind of energy on me and I couldn't pretend I was something I wasn't."[81]

"I knew that I wasn't going to be content to stay home, and I knew that a career was very much in my future," she said. "Lane said he wanted to have a family and I said no. If I did have a baby, that baby would have to be the whole thing for me. That was not my field of expertise, so I decided not to have children. In those days, people just didn't understand that as well as they do now."[82]

After just a year, the couple separated over their disagreement about a family—and another year later, divorced for good in 1951. Betty again moved back home, but this time edging near age 30.

"I was ashamed to tell anyone I had moved back home," she said. "You really feel like you've flunked the course, it's a terrible, self-defeating feeling. I failed, it's not anyone else's fault. And with Lane, it was my failure. It was my failure to not live up to being the kind of wife he wanted."[83]

Perhaps it was her shame, or fear of failure a third time, but Betty stayed single—this time for nearly a decade until a 1961 appearance as a panelist on the TV game show *Password* changed her life forever.

"There was no way I wanted to get married again, I was happily single, had boyfriends and was committed to my career," she said.[84]

Years later, Betty said she had no regrets about having no children.

"I made a very conscious decision not to have children, which was rather unheard of at the time," Betty told a reporter in 1986. "I love children, and if there are kids around, we will migrate together, then I go home and they go home, which is fine with me. I just didn't feel like it would be fair to try to make a split between my life and my career."[85]

She said others continually warned her that she would someday regret not having her own children. "I never have," she said. "I haven't regretted it for a minute."[86]

Betty had one other serious romance in her life that didn't result in marriage—she dated Army Air Corps Colonel Philip G. Cochran for more than four years, before breaking it off. First introduced to Cochran by *Tonight Show* host Jack Paar, Paar recalled that "they met, they fell in love . . . and I thought they would get married, but he wanted her to live on a farm and raise horses, but she wanted to stay in Hollywood and be a star."[87]

Paar recalls that "Phil sent Betty something when she announced she was going to marry Allen (Ludden). He sent a wire—it was one word, 'Ouch.'"[88]

Enter Leading Man: Allen Ludden

It's not as if Betty stood much of a chance against the determined Allen Ludden, an educated and well-spoken man and the host of one of TV's most popular shows, *Password* (at that time broadcast as a primetime game show). Ludden's star was rising as fast as Betty's. Betty appeared as a celebrity panelist on Ludden's popular *Password* series during its first season in 1961, and it was love at first sight—at least for Ludden.

Betty called Ludden "the salesman of all time" working on her for more than a year to get her to say "yes" to his marriage proposal.

"If you get down to the nitty-gritty, I was either never going to see Allen again or make a commitment," she said.[89]

It seems Ludden knew that Betty was for him from the start—game show pioneer Bob Stewart told Betty many years later that after her first appearance as a panelist on *Password,* Ludden came back to the production office and declared, "I am going to marry that woman someday."[90]

Allen Ludden was born October 5, 1918 in tiny Mineral Point, Wisconsin, about 200 miles northwest and four years before Betty's own birth in the Chicago hamlet of Oak Park, Illinois. Often referred to as "the happy highbrow," Ludden's professorial manner made him a natural for early TV panel and game show entries such as *General Electric Presents the College Bowl*, and later many, many iterations of the wildly successful *Password* game show.

Ludden's career finished far from where it started—as a high school English teacher in Austin, Texas in 1941 just after receiving undergraduate and graduate degrees from the University of Texas. After military service in World War II, Ludden gave up teaching and worked for a short time as a talent agent, and as a radio announcer. His work in early 1940s radio led to stage performances that took him from Texas to Connecticut, and eventually to New York.

In 1953, executives at General Electric were looking for just the right host for their new "reality" show (before shows were ever called that), known as *General Electric Presents the College Bowl*. It was during this stint he met a production assistant named Grant Tinker, a man who was to become very important in both Allen and Betty's lives.

Ludden stayed in New York for several years, including new opportunities offered by WCBS Radio. In 1959, *College Bowl* moved to a new medium, TV—and Ludden was an instant hit. He also worked for a time as a "voice coach" for famed CBS News notables Harry Reasoner and Charles Kuralt.

By 1961, Ludden was recruited to host the new *Password*—an early game show effort by eventual TV game show icons Mark Goodson and Bill Todman. The show ran for more than 1,500 episodes on daytime TV and another 1,000 episodes in a primetime format on CBS. *Password* was simple, but challenging where contestants were brought on the show and pared with one of two celebrity guests for the week. Short, succinct clues were required in order for the playing partner to guess the correct password.

While Betty and Allen's on-camera interactions were positive and reflected the erudite nature of the show, Ludden was going through a major life change. Off camera, his wife Margaret was in the final stages of a painful death from cancer and finally succumbed on October 31, 1961. Ludden, now a single, widowed father of three, faced a void in his life. In time, it would be Betty who would fill in the void.

In 1962, Betty and Ludden were both cast in the Ira Levin's three-act comic play, "Critics' Choice," for summer stock performances in Connecticut and Maine. The time together that summer further cemented Ludden's feelings for Betty.

Ludden's long and determined courtship of Betty enlisted the help of one of his oldest friends—Grant Tinker. Along with Tinker's famous wife Mary Tyler Moore (co-starring at the time as Laura Petrie on CBS' *Dick Van Dyke Show*), Ludden asked for the couple's help.

"Grant and I were auditioning Betty on behalf of Allen Ludden," Moore recalls. "Allen said, 'I want you to meet her and I really hope you like her because I really, really like her.'"[91]

Moore recalls she and Tinker were polite to Betty, "but we were making mental notes—we noted that she held Allen's hand, that was a good point, but we also noted she laughed too hard at one of his jokes. It was just crazy that we did that to each other. But we loved (Betty) immediately, and how could you not?"[92]

Tinker recalls that "Allen was quite smitten with her, and they had a lot in common. Allen was kind of a straight-laced guy, and Betty, is Betty. She can play anything from a nun to a trollop, and I think Allen was just thrilled by her outspoken humor, and he fell deeply in love. I am not sure Betty fell, however, as quickly as he did." [93]

Moore recalls being astonished that Betty turned down Ludden's first marriage proposals. "How could she turn down such a delightful, handsome and bright man?" Moore asked.[94]

Marriage and Kids

Betty finally relented, and stopped making Allen ask for her hand. The couple married at long last on June 14, 1963 in a civil ceremony at the Sands Hotel-Casino in Las Vegas. Ludden's three children and Betty's parents served as witnesses, and the couple took a brief honeymoon trip to Laguna Beach, California.

For Betty, it meant a huge lifestyle change. Not only would she have to grow to know her new husband by living with him for the first time, but also his three teenage children—David, Martha and Sarah. An instant step-mother, Betty said the role "required adjustments on all sides."

She struggled at first—especially when she would try to back-up Ludden in his parenting (for example, saying no when he had told the kids no), but then was frustrated to find Ludden eventually changed his "no" to "yes"—leaving Betty has the "evil step mom."

While Ludden brought three teenage children to the marriage—Betty brought her own kids—two poodles. It was a smart move—children, especially teenagers, Betty noted, can be fickle in their day-to-day affections for their father. Poodles never are—they always love it when you come home.

The couple never had any of their own children—Betty explaining in interviews that she was "committed to her career" and "I love kids, and I still enjoy them like mad, but I think I would be a terribly compulsive mother. That would be my whole focus and I didn't think I would do a good job of that."[95]

"Life does not come equipped with an instruction manual, and neither does death," Betty said. "Allen and I had worked together on and off during almost 18 years of marriage, but in our private life we were always very much a team."

She adds, "As well as lovers, we were each other's critic, editor, fan and friend."[96]

"Allen taught me what marriage was all about," Betty said. "I should not have ever gotten married before. I was happily single for many years and I was sold on the idea of marriage with Allen as a nice place to live. It was, it was just wonderful."[97]

Betty thinks Allen's on-camera success was based on the fact that he was real. "He was just like you saw, what you saw with him is what you got," she said. "I think I fell in love with his enthusiasm. He was interested in everything. He could talk into the camera and be so natural and so much like himself, you have to fall in love with someone like that."[98]

A Long Good-Bye

The first anyone (outside of the close circle of friends Betty and Allen kept) knew of a serious illness slowly overtaking Ludden's active life came in October 1980 when he suffered what was reported as a debilitating stroke while the couple visited the site of their new home under construction overlooking the Pacific Ocean in Carmel, California. Then just 62-years-old, Ludden was reported to have suffered "a massive stroke" and remained in a coma in critical condition with Betty at his side.[99]

Five days later came news that Ludden had come out of his coma and was removed from the hospital's critical list. Fred Sorri, a spokesman for Monterey Community Hospital, told reporters that Ludden was "talking to his nurses and is identifying them by name" and continued to make improvement. Days later came even more good news—Ludden was up on his feet and beginning to exercise, doing physical therapy, and sitting up in his bed watching *Password* on TV (with fellow game show emcee Tom Kennedy filling in as host). Although his long-term prognosis was listed as "guarded," he was finally released from the Monterey hospital 22 days after suffering the stroke, and transferred to the Good Samaritan Hospital in Los Angeles where he could be treated by his own doctor. He finally was allowed to return to the couple's Brentwood home on November 15, 1980.[100]

Betty and Allen had made a deliberate effort to keep news of Ludden's terminal illness away from family, friends and fans. Both kept working in television as they always had. "What's the point of going public?" Betty asked. "In their love and sorrow, our friends would be killing him off two years before he died. We didn't want to negate what was really quality time for both of us. We had no guilts or blames. It was just a bum break."[101]

By January 1981, Betty and Allen were ready to state publicly what was behind the physical challenges. "The good Lord and Betty White got me out of it, and I'm going to live because of her," Ludden told *Los Angeles Times* reporter Yardena Arar. "I'm planning very much to go back on the air. But whether or not I stay on the air, I don't know."[102]

Ludden disclosed his previously reported "stroke" was actually a coma induced by his growing struggle with cancer. The coma, he said, was caused by "a super-high calcium count, which should have killed me." While not providing specific details, Ludden confirmed his struggles were cancer related and that he was forgoing chemotherapy and radiation treatments.[103]

Ludden's positive approach—telling a reporter he was drinking water to flush his system of any harmful levels of calcium—was short-lived. On June 9, 1981, just slightly more than six months since coming home from the hospital, Ludden was gone. News reports indicated he died "after a long battle with cancer" and that Betty "was at his side when he died at 1:25 p.m. PDT at Good Samaritan Hospital" in Los Angeles.[104]

Betty's publicist, Larry Bloustein, confirmed for reporters that Ludden had battled cancer for almost two years and that a malignancy had been removed from his abdomen during a surgery in 1980.

"We were so lucky that he didn't go through a lot of pain," Betty said. "He didn't have a lot of pain, it was more that he just gradually faded. I was always grateful for that."[105]

It was during this stint in the hospital that Betty took a phone call at a nurse's station outside Allen's room—it was her friend Mary Tyler Moore calling to break the news that her only son, 24-year-old Richie Meeker, had died in a gun accident.

"Mary called me after Midnight and I can still see myself standing at the nurse's station outside Allen's room," Betty said. "Mary and I finally let it all hang out with each other. Until then, we had always held something back. But we were both crying and talking about the two people we loved."[106]

In the days before he died, Ludden's friends Tinker and Moore showed up together (despite their marital separation), effectively lifting his spirits.

"Allen had been trying to get us back together," Moore said. "And so we just went there and sat with him and acted like everything was fine. Allen was beaming. He was so happy to see us together, and he knew, he just knew everything was going to be like it once had been. But of course, it wasn't, but he didn't know that."[107]

Ludden had hoped to return to host *Password* in 1980-81, its 20th year on television, but it was not to be. In an earlier interview in what would be the final weeks of his life, he told a reporter that "I've been on television for about 20 years, and I just did my job. But the mail that I have had, the prayers I've had said—I start to cry every time I talk about it . . . You just don't realize how many people can really relate to you and care about you."[108]

In addition to Betty, Ludden was survived by the three children from his first marriage, and his elderly mother in Texas. Organized by his friend Grant Tinker, Ludden's private funeral was well-attended by many Hollywood friends at the Church of the Hills at Forrest Lawn Memorial Park in Los Angeles. He was buried in Graceland Cemetery in his home town of Mineral Point, Wisconsin.

Betty said in the years after Allen's death she would still talk to him inside their homes in Brentwood and Carmel. She said her beloved husband left her a very long letter that she treasured more and more in the years after his death. In it, he explained once again the depth and nature of his love for Betty. "He told me things (in the letter) that you need to hear again," she said.[109]

"While we had two long years to get used to the idea, when he died I was shattered," Betty said. "My first instinct was to crawl away somewhere to mourn in private, and to some extent, I suppose I did."[110]

Betty told Barbara Walters many years later that she really never "got over" Allen's death, "but you have to keep busy. They can't hit a moving target."[111]

She reminisces often about their personal time at the end of long days in show business, sipping vodka cocktails, Allen cooking on the grill, and Betty doing her needlepoint. She even recalls Allen putting a record on and the two of them enjoying dancing quietly all alone.

Seven years after Ludden's death, in late March 1988, Betty and a small group of family and friends gathered on the famed Hollywood Walk of Fame to unveil Ludden's star—the 1,868th such star to be placed—situated next to Betty's own star. The public plaza in front of the Koala Castle at the Los Angeles Zoo was also renovated and named for Ludden.

"I could hear his voice saying 'I can't believe it,'" White said to those assembled. "I cannot express what this day means to me."[112]

Tears almost always near the surface, Betty turned quickly and added a funny line: "Don't be surprised if in the wee hours of the morning, our (two) stars are fooling around," she said.[113]

Just four years after Ludden's passing, Betty dealt with death of her 87-year-old mother Tess, who had come to live in Betty's Brentwood, California home in her final years. "We were so close, we couldn't get any closer," Betty said. "Physically, she just went away."[114]

Betty believes the statement some offer that one never feels old until their mother dies—then you are no one's baby. "I did feel older (when she died), but an actress is like a ballplayer; she can't get old or be a grown-up. Otherwise, she can't hit the ball. My mother would have hated me to get old, and fortunately, she got to know *The Golden Girls* was a success before she died."[115]

Betty said she has been asked many times why she didn't remarry after Ludden's death. "Allen's been gone, can you believe it, for (more than) 25 years. I say, when you've had the best, who needs the rest," she told Bonnie Hunt during a 2008 interview.[116]

Inside the Actors Studio host James Lipton hosted Betty in 2010 and ran her through his traditional final questions (inspired by French personality Bernard Pivot) about her favorite and least favorite words, and other topics. Upon being asked what she wanted to hear God say as she approached the gates of Heaven, Betty replied, "Come on in, Betty, here's Allen!"[117]

4

—————————

FROM *MARY* TO *MAMA*

THE MOORE–THE MARY-IER

If Betty was anything in Hollywood, she was a good judge of what parts would work, and which ones wouldn't. Although she has appeared in just about every show possible—and not all of them were hits—she has shown an uncanny ability to pick the right part.

"I've learned that actors are just part of the process," Betty said. "It's all about the writing. If it's not on the page, it's not going to work."[118]

She noted joining the cast of *The Mary Tyler Moore Show* was easy—the show had been on the air for four seasons before Sue Ann Nivens showed up. *The Golden Girls*, her later and perhaps even bigger success, was harder to size up.

Professionalism, Betty said, is the most important part of her job on any set.

"It's not about you, it's about everyone," she said. "Don't take yourself too seriously. Come to the set prepared and don't act like you know more than anyone else or you're more important than anyone else in the production."[119]

It is good advice—and some she followed perhaps too closely for at least one co-star.

Betty recalls her first day on *The Mary Tyler Moore Show* set and co-star Valerie Harper's whisper to the show's star: "Look, she's got all her lines memorized. She's already memorized all her lines!"

It wasn't that Betty was trying to show up anyone—it just reflected her desire to be as prepared as possible, and not to disappoint her dear friend Mary who was giving her a guest spot on her hit show.

Betty need not have worried. "She was so good, she knocked their socks off," Moore said. "They decided right there and then that she was going to be a regular character on the show."[120]

Moore's other half at home and at MTM Enterprises, Grant Tinker, agreed.

"I cannot imagine anyone else coming into a situation like that, where we had a group together for four years already, and we really had that (show) going like a machine," Tinker said. "To become another cog in the machine and to do it brilliantly, that's what she did."[121]

Co-star Edward Asner, earning high praise for his own portrayal of Mary's boss Lou Grant, dubbed Betty "a party crasher" but quickly adds, "But boy, did she fit in."[122]

Moore thinks Betty worked so well on the show because of her natural ability to be real, and to be funny. "She's so funny, but it's always based on truth, based on her observations, which don't miss the mark by very much, ever," Moore said.[123]

For Betty, being on *The Mary Tyler Moore Show* represented some of "the best times" in her life. Her husband Allen would come to all the show's taping sessions on Friday nights,

It was a big night at the 28th Annual Television Academy of Arts & Sciences Awards—or the Emmy's—as four members of the cast of CBS' groundbreaking *Mary Tyler Moore Show* walked away with statuettes. Pictured backstage at the May 1976 awards with Betty from left are Edward Asner, Mary Tyler Moore, and Ted Knight. Although a co-star on *MTM*, Asner's Emmy came for his role in an ABC miniseries, *Rich Man, Poor Man*. *(AP Photo/Reed Saxon)*

and the two of them would then go off for a late dinner somewhere in Hollywood with Grant Tinker and the star's show, Mary Tyler Moore.

Things could not stay the same however—as divorce and disease eventually surfaced changing the "best of times" into some of the worst of times. But that was to come later, for now the family of MTM rode the wave of ratings success and critical acclaim with delight.

MTM: THE CRITICS & FEMINISTS' CHOICE

TV historians Harry Castleman and Walter Podrazik examined the significance of *The Mary Tyler Moore Show* for its era, and the unusually successful arrival of Betty. As they noted, the arrival of the Sue Ann Nivens character "provided yet another frontal attack on television's glossy self-image. White, drawing on her background of playing goody two-shoes characters over the years, portrayed the sweet-talking pure-as-gold 'women's show' star as a forked-tongue dirty old lady who merely used her bill-and-coo voice to mask the venom of her pointed remarks."[124]

The Mary Tyler Moore Show remains one of television critics' and viewers favorites. Feminists and other academic researchers have looked to the show for its commentary about its time, and the role of gender in society. Author Bonnie J. Dow noted that "if television scholars had established a cannon of 'great works' akin to what exists (although not without challenge) in literature, *The Mary Tyler Moore Show* surely would be included in it."[125]

Dow believes the show's "claim to originality" is based on several factors, including its outstanding production values, the fact that it was presented by a production company co-operated by a woman (MTM Enterprises), its focus on moving situation comedy away from "domestic or home-based situations to situations based in the workplace," and its "sensitivity and timeliness as a program focused on the life of a career-minded, single woman."[126]

The Mary Tyler Moore Show is generally acknowledged as the first popular and long-running television series to clearly feature the influence of feminism, Dow believes. "Although the show's creators consistently claimed that Mary's show was about characters, not politics . . . Mary (was presented) with the background of a world where women's rights were talked about and were having an impact."[127]

Betty said she felt honored to be a part of the Moore show, one she considered one of TV's all-time best.

"*The Mary Tyler Moore Show* was the first good effort as an ensemble cast," Betty said. "The show worked because they would slowly add in characters. If the character worked, they stayed. You can't get that kind of chemistry if you cast everybody in the first episode, and then everybody has to get a little piece and be in every show, and you really don't get to know them."[128]

If one needs evidence of the strength of the ensemble cast, TV historians Castleman and Podrazik note that six of the show's main characters—Ed Asner (*Lou Grant*, CBS), Valerie Harper (*Rhoda*, CBS; *Valerie*, NBC), Cloris Leachman (*Phyllis*, CBS; *Malcolm in the Middle* and *Raising Hope*, both Fox), Ted Knight *(Too Close for Comfort*, ABC), Gavin MacLeod (*The Love Boat*, ABC) and of course Betty—all went on to highly successful careers in subsequent series. In fact, the only regular member of the cast who struggled in the post-MTM years was Mary. Mary faltered in her biggest post *MTM* effort, a short-lived 1978 variety showed titled *Mary* that was dropped by CBS at mid-season due to low ratings.

Betty credits the show's writers. "It is terrible to say that there are not good writers around anymore—but (television) is a voracious medium. Television eats up a lot of material like it can't get it fast enough and it takes a lot of cleverness to keep manipulating things that are funny and fresh."[129]

Although the Moore show had a stable of brilliant and creative writers—among them Jim Brooks, Allen Burns, Stan Daniels, Ed Weinberger, and David Lloyd—Betty credits Lloyd with getting the character of Sue Ann "in his teeth and really running with it, he made her as evil as she was."[130]

Both Betty and the show's star, Mary Tyler Moore, make an important distinction about the writing and production of the show. Betty said Mary would call the writers on "going for the easy laugh."

Moore would tell the show's writers, "'that's too sketchy. That's not character humor,' and she was right. Character humor was what made it work. What's funny is the way the character reacts to what is said or done, not the line itself," Betty said.[131]

The critics agree. "Even though the talented cast was the driving force behind the success of *The Mary Tyler Moore Show*, the high level of sophistication in the show's scripts lifted the series above the restrictive confines TV sitcoms were proscribed into during the 1960s," Castleman and Podrazik declare.[132]

Memorable Sue Ann Moments

It's well established that a lucky strike of lightning propelled Betty into the cast of the hit CBS comedy, *The Mary Tyler Moore Show*, in 1973. The role of Sue Ann Nivens, "The Happy Homemaker," was one many actors would have relished (excuse the food pun), but few could have made as much of the role as Betty did.

Appearing in 39 total episodes between 1973 and the series end in 1977, Betty was front and center for 10 episodes, all of them creating memorable moments worth recalling.

 SEASON 4

The Lars Affair—Originally aired September 15, 1973
Here's where it all started. Betty was listed as a "Guest Star" on an early fall episode in 1973, with recurring cast member Cloris Leachman as Phyllis listed as a "Special Guest Star." A classic showdown was in store.

The audience didn't seem to mind that it was the beginning of the end for Phyllis Lindstrom's character on Mary's show—she was soon to be off and running on her own CBS spin-off, *Phyllis*, that eventually aired for two seasons from 1975-77.

This particular show opened with one of Mary's familiar— but not always successful parties. As everyone (except Mary) seems to know: Her parties stink.

As Sue Ann breezes through the room, Phyllis turns to Mary and asks: "Who's Little Bo Peep?"

Mary's pal Rhoda (played by Valerie Harper) apparently is equally unimpressed and adds: "I love her dimples. I wonder if she made 'em herself?"

Sue Ann made a big impression very quickly. As she gathers her coat to leave, she regrets she won't be around to help Mary clean-up after the party. Sue Ann does have a suggestion, of course: "Now if you want to tidy up in a hurry, think of your room as a big clock. Start at Midnight, and go around the room clockwise and you'll be done in two shakes of a lamb's foot."

Surprisingly, never-seen character Dr. Lars Lindstrom offers Sue Ann a ride home from Mary's party—something his wife Phyllis knows nothing about. After more than two hours and Lars still hasn't returned from giving Sue Ann a ride, Phyllis is boiling. Lars does call on the phone and reports "a terrible accident" where the fender on his car has been damaged. Luckily, he and Sue Ann had the crash adjacent to an all-night auto body repair shop—so he'll be home after the repairs are done!

Phyllis buys Lars' story full of holes, but Mary and Rhoda don't. Mary is amazed, after all, "I mean, Sue Ann just doesn't seem like the type. She seems more like the type a man leaves for another woman!"

Mary is put in a tough spot—Phyllis eventually figures out that Lars is cheating on her with the sickly-sweet Sue Ann. "Since he's started seeing her, he's gained nine pounds, and his clothes are cleaner when he comes home than when he leaves!" Phyllis laments. Phyllis even confronts Sue Ann backstage at the WJM studios, getting her revenge by sabotaging a highly delicate soufflé that Sue Ann was making for her audience.

Mary finally steps in and zeroes right in on Sue Ann's ego. She threatens to expose Sue Ann's affair—"not a good image for the Happy Homemaker"—and as expected, Sue Ann picks her TV show over Lars. "I'm not doing it for myself, you see, but for all the ladies out there who *need* me," Sue Ann says.

Daytime TV and Minneapolis housewives are saved!

Just two months later, Sue Ann was back—again as a guest at one of Mary's parties. From there on, Sue Ann was a permanent member of the MTM ensemble.

Betty liked to laugh: "Sue Anne may have not been a very nice woman, but she was a very good home economist."[133]

SEASON 4

The Co-Producers—Originally aired January 19, 1974
Things are going great for Mary when WJM's station manager green lights her idea to produce a Sunday afternoon talk show—at least one episode. The station management, however, puts a kink in Mary's plans by insisting that Channel 12's two established "stars," news anchorman Ted Baxter (brilliantly cast with blithering comic Ted Knight) and "The Happy Homemaker" Sue Ann Nivens, be slated as hosts of the show. "Talk of the Town," apparently an idea that Rhoda thought of first, gets underway with Mary and Rhoda agreeing to be co-producers.

That's the last agreement anyone has, as arguments ensue immediately. First, Ted and Sue Ann can't agree on whose name should be listed first in the show's credits. Their egos get in the way even further when they take up the idea of the opening episode focusing on biographical sketches of both of the hosts. Sue Ann recalls she wants hers to start by telling the story of "a frightened, but darling" six-year-old child who wins a baby-talent contest impersonating Shirley Temple.

When Rhoda declares the "bio" segments "a dumb idea," Ted and Sue Ann walk out. (Rhoda didn't know that Ted can't stand the word "dumb" being used in the same sentence as his name.)

Ted and Sue Ann are willing to come back, but want Mary to fire Rhoda from the show. Eventually, Mary says if Rhoda goes, she goes. Ted and Sue Ann like that idea a lot. "After all, how hard can it be to find a producer!" Sue Ann declares.

 **SEASON 5**

A New Sue Ann—Originally aired October 26, 1974

Linda Kelsey—later of *Lou Grant*, guest stars as Gloria Munson—an "All about Eve" up and comer who has set her sights on Sue Ann's world.

This is also an early episode where we see Sue Ann's lust for news director Lou Grant come into full flourish. When Sue Ann describes her feelings for Lou, Mr. Grant asks: "Why does everything you say sound like food?"

"Oh fudge!" Sue Ann replies.

There's more hot fudge in store for Sue Ann as the new WJM station manager thinks the "Happy Homemaker Show" needs improvement. Desperate, Sue Ann asks Lou for advice for how to deal with the station manager. Lou notes that the manager had always liked the ladies. It's an idea Sue Ann is ready to embrace: "Dear Lou. Dear cryptic, bashful, dirty-minded Lou . . . I guess I do owe him at least the courtesy of listening to his vile suggestions."

Mary introduces the Gloria character who summarily gushes over Sue Ann as her all-time favorite TV personality. Sue Ann says to Mary, "I don't believe I've met this adorable, and perceptive youngster!" Sue Ann quickly hires Gloria as her stand-in and "gal Friday."

Sealing the deal, Gloria's confesses that she's watched "The Happy Homemaker" over and over, even in reruns, and says, "I even know your dumplings by heart."

News writer Murray Slaughter (biting deadpan character actor Gavin MacLeod) can't resist and adds, "Who doesn't?!"

Back on the "Happy Homemaker" set, Gloria quickly moves in on Sue Ann's territory—thinking up the idea of demonstrating exercises housewives can do at home. When they appear to be too strenuous for Sue Ann to undertake, Gloria quickly steps in to demonstrate them—and Sue Ann is relegated to just describing the exercises. Soon Sue Ann's role is cut out altogether.

Gloria:	"I wonder what I should do for my first exercise on the show?"
Sue Ann:	"What about a head stand?"
Gloria:	"You just want me to stand on my head?"
Sue Ann:	"No, I want to stand on *your* head."

It doesn't take long—in three days Gloria is off to lunch and dinner with the station manager and he's consulting her about all aspects of Sue Ann's show. Mary asks Sue Ann why she is so worried that her getting so close to the station manager necessarily means Gloria is going to her job. Sue Ann replies, "How do you think I got it?!"

Soon the station manager gives Gloria her own baking segment on the show. "Perhaps he has a weakness for tarts," Sue Ann declares.

Sue Ann gets the last laugh—she spikes the baked creations from Gloria, and the whole station (including Sue Ann) comes down with food poisoning.

What Are Friends For?—Originally aired November 16, 1974
Once he learns love (or is that lust?) sick Sue Ann plans to attend the annual broadcasters' convention in Chicago— Lou is no longer interested in representing WJM at the conference. Sue Ann plans to go because Chicago is where she had her first cooking show, "Let's Talk about Meat."

Lou tells Mary to go, and unfortunately, Mary and Sue Ann end up with adjoining rooms. It also means Mary gets free "helpful" hints: "Mary, don't forget, put your slacks under the mattress, so while we sleep we also press our pants!"

Mary's plans for a quiet time at the convention are quickly interrupted—Sue Ann goes out and finds some friendly conventioneers—morticians—staying in the same hotel. When Mary is not up for Sue Ann's plans with the just-met friends, she refuses to go along. Sue Ann notes, "Mary, stubbornness is the biggest weed in our garden."

Mary finally gives in—and goes to dinner—and the morticians promptly shower Mary with all the attention, much to Sue

Ann's chagrin. Hurt feelings or not, Sue Ann gets in a good dig: "Mary, doesn't it bother you that you were the favorite of men who spend all their time with dead people?"

Eventually, the girls dump the morticians and Sue Ann opens up about all the rejection she's felt while dating and begins to cry, "You know what I hate most about crying? Your dimples don't show."

 ## SEASON 6

Mary's Delinquent—Originally aired November 1, 1975
Mary is a new volunteer for the Big Sisters program, which brings guest star MacKenzie Phillips (later on another CBS hit, *One Day at a Time*) as Mary's "delinquent" girl.

In the same show, Sue Ann is nominated for "Twin Cities TV Woman of the Year" and needs an updated resume. She asks Murray to type it. "You know I can't type with these long, beautiful nails."

Murray says, "Oh, I always thought they were retractable."

Sue Ann needs to pad her resume and asks, "What other kind, selfless things have I done to aid mankind?"

Murray says, "Did you include the time the Shriner's were in town?"

"Oh Murray, I'm going to let that remark go now, and hurt you very deeply, later."

Sue Ann decides to join Mary in the Big Sisters program. "Oh, I'd be perfect for that. I was always a wonderful sister. I was so kind, I had to be, after all, it was my sister who was the ugly one."

Sue Ann pops in with her new little sister—declaring, "I have a little sister too! But mine's black!" Sue Ann quickly picks up "street lingo" using words like "bad," "threads," "we all boogie to a different drummer," dons a blonde afro, and attends a double-feature movie featuring *Shaft* and *Superfly*.

"Oh, it was wonderful watching them sticking it to the honkies!" she declares.

Mary and Sue Ann decide to put their two young sisters together for a luncheon. Sue Ann announces, "You two (girls) should have a lot in common. She's a delinquent too!"

A problem quickly arises, though, as Mary's protégé is the prime suspect in the case of some missing money from a desk in the WJM newsroom. Mary wants to get to the bottom of things her own way, but Sue Ann tells Mary, "Oh please let me help. (Young people) always relate better to someone closer to their own age!"

Sue Ann's plans don't work out—but Lou comes to the rescue and Mary's "little sister" returns the money.

The Happy Homemaker Takes Lou Home—Originally aired Dec. 6, 1975
Sue Ann's dream finally comes true in this episode. But it wasn't without some outside help.

"Oh Lou! You're just like chicken Kiev. A crusty shell, but all soft and runny on the inside," Sue Ann declares.

Sue Ann tells Mr. Grant that she's certain of how attracted he is to her because he goes to such lengths to hide it. "See, you're afraid that the little pilot light of love that is within you might flicker and ignite your whole oven!"

Sue Ann seeks out Mary's help in getting Lou to agree to come to her house for dinner. She goes to Mary's apartment late at night, waking Mary. "Oh Mary dear, I hope I haven't disturbed you."

Mary says, "Well, I was in bed."

Sue Ann: "Oh good, than that means you are alone."

In a moment of weakness and desperate to get Sue Ann and her bum date out of her apartment at 2 a.m., Mary agrees to help.

When Lou finally goes to dinner at Sue Ann's she compliments his appetite—"you had second and thirds of everything."

"Well, I was just trying to make the meal last," he said, revealing he is afraid of what comes next. *What comes next* is a full-court press by Sue Ann to finally, finally bed her one true lust: Lou Grant.

Lou convinces Sue Ann to back down. "The treasure doesn't have to go looking for the hunter. You've got it all turned around, Sue Ann."

He finally tells her "you're a treasure, you should act like it."

A philosophical Sue Ann notes, "Isn't life funny, I've been accepted by a bunch of guys, and felt awful. You just rejected me and I feel like a million dollars. Thank you, Lou."

Once I Had a Secret Love—Originally aired January 17, 1976
Mr. Grant arrives on a Monday morning in "one of his moods"—but no one is going to believe what has put him in that kind of mood.

Declaring he wants Mary to remove all liquor from his office, Lou confides that "I do stupid things I regret when I have liquor." He then confesses he got drunk and woke up the next morning in Sue Ann's bedroom.

Although it's not specifically stated (rather implied in this, 1970s primetime) that Lou and Sue Ann had sex, Lou is worried that Sue Ann will now expect him to marry her.

Mary says, "Oh c'mon, Mr. Grant, she's not going to make you marry her. What do you expect her to do, hold a spatula to your throat?"

Moments later Sue Ann enters the newsroom and utters one of her most famous lines: "I didn't sleep a wink all night. I feel wonderful!"

Mary promises not to tell anyone about the Lou-Sue Ann hook-up, but Murray starts badgering Mary to tell her what was wrong with Mr. Grant.

Later, Sue Ann's hairdresser tells Ted Baxter that "there's a new man in Sue Ann's life. What kind of dumbo would want to hang out with Sue Ann? Either he's a glutton for punishment, or he just got out of prison."

Just as Ted thinks he's getting close to figuring it out, Sue Ann bursts in and says, "Oh Lou, I just wanted to give you your socks back." Ted still doesn't get it, however. Murray does and later violates Mary's confidence. Lou is not happy, and reduces Mary to tears saying, "I'm your boss, but we're not friends anymore."

Lou later tries to apologize to Sue Ann if he's taken advantage of her. She's having none of it and replies, "Lou you were wonderful. If you were a soufflé, you would raise high in the pan! If you were a crepe Suzette, your flame would light a whole room."

Lou eventually forgives Mary—a happy ending. (And he agrees to two dinners and a lunch with Sue Ann!)

Sue Ann Falls in Love—Originally aired February 28, 1976
Everyone in the WJM newsroom is excited about local Television Editors Awards—the "Teddy" awards—that find Ted nominated (answering his prayers), Murray finally nominated for a news writing award, and Sue Ann Nivens getting a nomination as well. The missing nomination: Mary!

Sue Ann introduces a new beau—an outdoorsman type named Doug—and gloats he's "been teaching me the adventures of the great outdoors. And I've been teaching him the adventures of the great *indoors*."

Sue Ann is so smitten, she dumps Lou as her escort to the "Teddy" awards ceremony.

"It's terrible that one has to break one man's heart to satisfy the desires of another man," Sue Ann said. "How lucky you are, Mary, that you won't *ever* have that problem."

Sue Ann tells Lou that her new beau Doug has "such an instinct for survival."

Lou replies: "That's good, he's gonna need it!"

Sue Ann tells Lou: "Someday you'll meet a beautiful, sexy woman who will help you forget all about me. In the meantime, why don't you take Mary to the awards ceremony?!"

Later in the episode, Mary gets in a rare back-slap to Sue Ann after Sue Ann gloats that she made her evening gown herself. "Oh, I'm surprised you were able to find that much fabric!"

Sue Ann tells Mary she's convinced she's in love with Doug because she screwed up the recipe for Hungarian goulash. "A half cup, a whole cup, who can be bothered, my cup is running over with love!"

Amidst over-the-top public displays of affection between Sue Ann and Doug, what Sue Ann doesn't know is—Doug's a lecherous creep—stealing a kiss from Mary when Sue Ann is out of the room.

When it's time for the "Teddy" awards dinner, Ted Baxter decides to save some money and rent his gal Georgette (actress Georgia Engel) a tux—"what's the sense of buying an evening gown for one night?"

Georgette resists compliments that they look cute in their matching tuxes by declaring, "I don't care what anybody says, I think we look like the top of a gay wedding cake!"

Sue Ann is sure she's going to win, and plans for an acceptance speech—including letting the audience enjoy her dimples for a few moments. The evening is almost ruined, however, as Mary finally lets Sue Ann know the truth about Doug. Her tears quickly vanish, however, as she wins the "Best Daytime Host" award.

SUE ANN UNTIL THE END

Two other notable episodes with Sue Ann at the center of the action included "Sue Ann's Sister" (originally aired October 9, 1976) and "Sue Ann Gets Fired" (January 29, 1977). In both episodes, Sue Ann's reign as the "queen of daytime TV" in Minneapolis is placed in doubt. In one episode, Sue Ann's sister Lila (actress Pat Priest) shows up to launch a rival show to Sue Ann's "Happy Homemaker."

It doesn't matter—weeks later WJM managers dump Sue Ann's show for good—but at least Mary saves the day by getting Lou to agree to add a "Helpful News Hints" segment to the WJM News.

Again, it's a short-lived opportunity as soon the entire newsroom staff (sans Ted Baxter) are fired by WJM portending the end of the memorable *Mary Tyler Moore Show*.

Two of Betty's co-stars, Gavin MacLeod who portrayed Murray and Edward Asner who brought us Lou Grant, have funny takes on the magic of Sue Ann.

MacLeod noted that "Sue Ann taught me things to do with a bald head that shouldn't even be mentioned!"

Asner remarked about his famous scene with Sue Ann where *she* tackles Lou on the sofa: "I got a hernia from that scene."[134]

"Sue Ann was such an interesting character," Betty said. "She was this sicky, yucky, sweet adorable gal as long as the red light was on, and the moment it went off she was a monster. And she also happened to be the neighborhood nymphomaniac."[135]

Betty still enjoys telling fans about her late husband Allen Ludden's take on the Sue Ann character: "The only difference between Betty and Sue Ann is that Betty can't cook![136]

The Mary Tyler Moore Show could not last forever—and the show came to a tearful ending (but with a final episode to wrap up story lines)—on March 19, 1977.

"That last week (of the show), we were all basket cases," Betty said. "The writers couldn't write that last scene. The last scene was missing until Wednesday. We read through it, blocked it and then walked away. And then when we rehearsed it we all went to pieces."

While Betty may think the Moore show had some more life in it—she could not argue with Moore's own decision to end the show after seven brilliant seasons. "It was a classic (show), and the writers ended it perfectly with Mary just closing the door and turning off the lights," Betty said.

The old MTM studio where the show was created each week—now known as CBS Radford Studios in Hollywood—

holds a plaque that reads: "On this stage, a company of loving and talented friends created a television classic, *The Mary Tyler Moore Show*."[137]

THE QUOTABLE SUE ANN NIVENS

Though her appearances stretched over several seasons, Betty's character of Sue Ann Nivens was not in every episode of *The Mary Tyler Moore Show*. Therefore, it's appropriate to review once again the very best of the highly quotable, and always memorable "Happy Homemaker" —

ON MINNEAPOLIS WEATHER

Sue Ann: "Snow always inspires such awe in me. Just consider one single snowflake alone, so delicate, so fragile, so ethereal. And yet when a billion of them come together through the majestic force of nature, they can screw up a whole city."

ON GIVING OUT THE SAME "OLD" HOUSEHOLD HINTS

Sue Ann: "Same old household hints? Do these sound like the same old household hints? Lemon juice your nick-nacks. New life for your squeegee. Moisten your suction cups. Kiss soap dish jelly good bye. Same old hints!"

ON PASSIONATE MOMENTS WITH LOU GRANT (OR JUST *ON TOP OF* LOU GRANT)

Sue Ann: "Go ahead Lou, you're stronger than me! Press your advantage! Be gentle, Lou, that's all I ask!" *(as she tries to pin Mr. Grant to the sofa)*

ON HER CRUSH ON LOU

(As Lou walks into the newsroom)

>   Lou: "OK, I've got it!"
>   Sue Ann: "I know, and I want it!"

ON RHODA'S FASHION SENSE

>   Sue Ann: "Oh Rhoda! I wish I could wear old clothes
>   as well as you do!"

ON MARY'S PROSPECTS FOR GETTING A MAN

>   Mary: "Guess what? I may be having Prince
>   Charles on my show."
>   Sue Ann: "Oh Mary, you and him would make a
>   wonderful pair, if only you weren't so old,
>   American and common."

ON MARY'S LOVE LIFE

>   Murray: "What are we doing out here? A woman is
>   giving birth in Mary's bedroom right now!"
>   Sue Ann: "Yes, I know. And it's probably the most
>   exciting thing that is *ever* going to happen in
>   there."

ON TRYING TO HELP DEAR, POOR MARY

>   Sue Ann: "Hello muckrakers! I just stopped by, Mary,
>   to make sure to tell you to stop by my
>   studio this week. I'm devoting an entire
>   week of shows to you poor, unfortunate
>   single girls."
>   Mary: "Sue Ann, in case you have forgotten, you
>   are single also."
>   Sue Ann: "Oh yes, but that's only because I don't
>   happen to place my love life above my
>   profession."
>   Murray: "I thought that was your profession?"
>   Sue Ann: "Oh Murray! Witty Murray! The jokes
>   fall from your lips—almost as fast as
>   the hair from your head!"

ON THE MORNING AFTER

Sue Ann: "I didn't sleep a wink all night. I feel wonderful!"

ON GETTING A LATE NIGHT IDEA

Sue Ann: "Mary, I was lying in bed last night and I couldn't sleep and I got the most wonderful idea. So I went right home and wrote it down!"

ON SEX AND VIOLENCE ON TV

Ted: "As far as I am concerned, there are two things that have no business on television: Sex and violence."

Sue Ann: "Oh! I never knew those were two different things."

ON WHAT TV NEEDS

Sue Ann: "I think television needs bright, young women. Look at me—and to a certain extent, Mary."

ON CRASHING THE MEN'S ROOM

Mary: "Sue Ann! Did you crash the men's room?"

Sue Ann: "Of course not! I went as somebody's guest."

ON SUE ANN'S SPREAD

Ted: "Hey Murray, did you notice this (newspaper) spread on Sue Ann?"

Murray: "Oh yeah, but you don't notice it so much when she sits down."

ON BEING PLOPPED DOWN ON A WEDDING CAKE BY MURRAY

Sue Ann: "It could use a little more vanilla."

ON SUE ANN'S BEDROOM

Sue Ann: "Oh Mary, if these walls could talk!"
Murray: "Sue Ann, I really love your bedroom. Did you decorate it yourself, or did you have a sex maniac come in?"
Sue Ann: "Very droll, Murray."

ON PUTTING MURRAY IN HIS PLACE

Sue Ann: "Dear Murray, with your sly wit it's a wonder you never become more successful!"

ON HER CHILDHOOD

Sue Ann: "I was a child prodigy. I was reading cook books at two, and I started pickling at six. When I was 12, I was quite heavily into sauces."

The All-New Betty White Show—Same Result

MTM and CBS executives reportedly had discussed the idea of "spinning off" the Sue Ann Nivens character while *The Mary Tyler-Moore Show* was still on the air (as they had done with *Rhoda* and *Phyllis*), but it wasn't until after the Moore show left the air that Betty got another shot at her own series. It was the latest attempt at *The Betty White Show* and premiered as part of the CBS fall-line up in September 1977. (There apparently was no need to call it *"The New" Betty White Show*, since the last one named that had left the air two decades earlier!)

Plunked into the prime 9 p.m. slot on CBS' Monday night lineup (just after *The Young Daniel Boone* and just before future co-star Bea Arthur's successful and sometimes controversial sitcom *Maude*), the show faced the growing reality that ABC's up-start *Monday Night Football* was en route to becoming a major TV franchise hit. While CBS had practically "owned" Monday nights for years with a series of successful comedies—including all of Lucille Ball's efforts on *I Love Lucy*, *The Lucy Show* and *Here's Lucy!*—by 1977, Betty had a tougher climb.

If anyone could catch the "rest" of the audience who didn't care for NFL football on a Monday night (after a Sunday schedule full of gridiron action on both CBS and NBC), CBS' comedy line-up of Betty and Bea showed promise. (NBC presumably hoped families would stick around for the *NBC Monday Movie* to run in the two-hour slot after its successful family lead-in, *Little House on the Prairie*.)

Betty's latest effort, perhaps mistakenly, left the popular Sue Ann Nivens character in the dumpster behind CBS Television City as her new show told the story of an aging, fictional actress "Joyce Whitman" trying to make a comeback in primetime in a series called "Undercover Woman." The premise was supposed to be a parody of NBC's successful Angie Dickinson vehicle, *Police Woman*. What the brain trust behind the show seemed to miss— no one viewed Betty as the sex pot Dickinson had become (what viewers today might call a "cougar").

TV historians Castleman and Podrazik noted that *The Betty White Show* fit the normal formula for a show from the MTM Studios—instead of an actual family, the ensemble cast was intended to create a "professional family of individuals who worked together and grew to love, respect, and depend on each other. Such an approach, however, needed time for the writers and the performers to develop the pacing of the series and for the audience to become familiar with the characters."[138]

Set up as "a show within a show," this version of *The Betty White Show* is still believed to be the only TV pilot featuring actors pretending to be making a TV pilot—basically a pilot within a pilot. The pilot episode also had the distinction of having been written by a very talented trio of TV writers—Ed Weinberger, Stan

Daniels and David Lloyd. The trio didn't stick around, however, as they moved on to develop *Taxi* over on ABC.

Betty said she didn't know the three were not planning to stay with her show. "I found that out after the fact, and I got the second team (of writers). The difference was horrendous."[139]

As Weinberger explained, "The first thing we considered, of course, was to transfer Sue Ann, 'The Happy Homemaker' to some suitable environment and simply let her career continue along her woman-hating, man-hungry, acerbic course." But Weinberger, White and CBS executives were worried that 30 minutes of Sue Ann may be too much to take—and may be too much like Cloris Leachman's spin-off show *Phyllis*—which had begun to slide in the ratings.[140]

Betty's take: "The only reason the character of Sue Ann worked at all was that sweet Mary tolerated her, and so the audience tolerated her. Without Mary, she would quickly get swamped in her own vinegar and become thoroughly unpleasant."[141]

Dead-pan actor John Hillerman co-starred in the series oddly as *both* Betty's ex-husband and as the persnickety director of "Undercover Woman." Betty's character enjoyed putting Hillerman down, calling him "old pickle puss," and other assorted barbs. Georgia Engle, a fellow alumnus from *The Mary Tyler Moore Show* (where she played anchorman Ted Baxter's wife Georgette) was Betty's pal "Mitzi" at home. An apparent grab for easy laughs included showing a bulky character "Hugo" as the blonde-wigged stunt double to Betty's "Joyce" character.

Betty had high hopes for the "Joyce Whitman" character and her new effort.

"[This character] is not as rotten as Sue Ann, she is a little better than that, but not an awful lot," Betty joked. "She doesn't start the trouble, but if someone zings her, she can handle herself and zing 'em right back."[142]

Betty said years later that she felt part of the reason the show failed was because "the audience was expecting Sue Ann Nivens. They weren't expecting Joyce Whitman."[143]

She contrasts her show's experience with another one produced in the same era by MTM Productions, *Lou Grant*, a successful CBS drama that ran from 1977-82 and pulled in 13 Emmy awards. The character of Lou Grant had changed from its portrayal on *The Mary Tyler Moore Show*—and the show's lead actor, Edward Asner, secured a full one-season contract with CBS, giving the show time to catch on with viewers.

Despite a heavy CBS promotional push and even a time slot switch to 9:30 p.m. to let Arthur's more successful *Maude* series to lead-off at 9 p.m., the "new" *Betty White Show* was to suffer the same fate as the earlier 1950s effort. CBS yanked the cord in January 1978 after just 14 episodes.

MTM and CBS had "tremendous hope" for Betty's new show for the 1977-78 season, and considered her show a "sure fire hit." The audience saw otherwise, despite efforts to carefully draw in the best elements of what had worked on *The Mary Tyler Moore Show*.

Ultimately, as Castleman and Podrazik posit, *The Betty White Show* "started strong in a tough spot (against *Monday Night Football* on ABC and an NBC movie), but then collapsed and was gone by January. Even with so many 'sure-fire' hooks , the mixture (on Betty's new show) had failed to gel, hurt chiefly by two flaws in the set-up: White's caustic character, while a good foil in a supporting role, did not provide a very likeable lead; and the angle of Joyce's former husband being the director of the fictional *Undercover Woman* series was a silly gimmick that just got in the way of the inevitable conflicts between the two working on opposite sides of the camera."[144]

CBS executives admitted privately, but later, that they canceled the show too soon, Betty said. "The executives wanted an instant ensemble (show), but they did stereotype, cartoon casting."[145]

Betty's primetime failure "was a great disappointment to MTM which had pegged the series as its front-line successor to Moore's Show," Castleman and Podrazik contend.[146]

Betty added, "I don't think the audience was ever quite ready for it, for the Joyce Whitman character, they were expecting Sue Ann." The cancelation left Betty feeling low—"I was devastated, heartbroken. It feels like such a failure."[147]

Roasting Betty

In the build-up to the September 1977 launch of *The Betty White Show*, her friend Dean Martin pulled together one of his celebrity TV bashes: *The Dean Martin Celebrity Roast*. Normally an affair for the "Man of the Hour," this version of Martin's roast from the MGM Grand Hotel in Las Vegas focused on the "Woman of the Hour." (The NBC special, produced under the Peacock network's long-term contract with Martin, was unusual in that it made numerous mentions of Betty's new show on CBS and featured several CBS primetime stars.)

"Betty's friends" who showed up to roast her included game-show host Peter Marshall, Jimmy "J.J." Walker from CBS' *Good Times*, Bonnie Franklin from CBS' *One Day at a Time*, Betty's new sit-com co-stars Georgia Engle and John Hillerman, Lawanda Page from NBC's *Sanford and Son*, Abe Vigoda from ABC's *Fish*, Dan Haggerty from NBC's *Grizzly Adams*, as well as Martin roast regulars Milton Berle, Red Buttons, Orson Wells, Phyllis Diller, Charley Callas, and Foster Brooks.

"They had this big long dais of all my 'closest friends,' most of whom I had never met," Betty said. "That's when I met Orson

Wells. Orson and I became friends after that. I looked at the dais and thought, 'One of my friends is Orson Wells?!'"[148]

The jokes were—well—a little stale and a little predictable.

Martin started things off by noting that Betty's former TV persona Sue Ann Nivens was so man-hungry, "a guard at the studio caught her passing out Hershey bars to the Osmond brothers."

He added, "When she first met Allen Ludden, she had to pretend she was shy. She would tell him, 'I can't make love with the lights on, so could you please close the car door?'"

Peter Marshall's forgettable best effort claimed that Betty was such an animal lover that she attended a dinner party recently where she insisted that each Animal Cracker in the house "be spayed and neutered."

Jimmy Walker noted he didn't know Betty well and asked his friend, *Roots* author Alex Haley about her, who confirmed that "like so many other people in America, Betty does have black roots."

In his regular bitterness about "never getting a roast," Red Buttons listed all of the other famous women in history who had never earned the honor given to Betty. Regardless, Buttons said "I am delighted to be here tonight for Betty White, a woman who once said to her husband Allen Ludden, 'Not tonight, unless you know the password."

Orson Wells said he was going to forgo the traditional rude remarks and coarse jokes, and instead offered his own poem:

Of all the lovely ladies on TV who grace our screens by night,
The last with class who steams my glass, is lovely Betty White.
Her lovely flowing gowns, her tailored suits, the way she fills her altereds,
Why she gets more front page scoops than Barbara Walters.
Yes, I've loved too long, so don't think that this is sudden,
For nothing stands between us now, except a man named Allen Ludden.

Lawanda Page, best known as the loud-mouthed Aunt Esther on *Sanford and Son*, broke up the panel by noting she had a hard time picking Betty out in the crowd. "You get a bunch of you albinos on one dais, and you all look alike to me!"

"To be honest with you, I don't even know why I'm at a dinner honoring Betty White," Page said in her classic edgy delivery. "Oh, but I'm just kidding, Betty. Of course your name is famous. They honor you all over the south. Over every drinking fountain there is a sign that says, 'White only.' "

She added, "I'm probably here because they couldn't get Farrah Fawcett."

Cosmetically-challenged Phyllis Diller was in regular form. She noted that "Betty has everything Miss America has, unfortunately, they served her the child's portion. If it wasn't for a hickey, she'd have no figure at all."

Diller noted that "Betty is a homebody—with a body like hers, she oughta stay home. A lot of people have complained about her posture. They say it always looks like she's sitting down. Not true—she's just short and dumpy."

Just as Diller played her part, so did Foster Brooks stumbling to the microphone in his trademark drunken schtick. "I remember the first time I laid eyes on old dimples here," Brooks said. "We were out on a blind date. She was out dating, and I was blind—drunk."

Milton Berle saved the night—noting that "I'm here tonight to honor Betty White, which should give you some idea of what is happening to my career."

He noted Betty had early success in show business—winning a dance contest at age 18 presenting "The Dance of the Virgin"— "which she performed from memory. Then she went on the road and traveled with the Tommy Dorsey Band. She wasn't a singer, she just liked to travel with the band."

The final speaker was one who actually knew Betty—her husband and *Password* host Allen Ludden (who was not seated on the dais with the other "stars" on hand).

Ludden noted the big role dogs play in Betty's life, noting that she would not accept his engagement ring until he sat up and begged. "And then on our honeymoon, she rolled over and played dead."

Ludden introduced Betty for her part of the roast as "Betty White Ludden"—a rare professional reference to her married name.[149]

Mama's Dearest: Daughter Ellen

Mama's Family, born of a successful series of skits on *The Carol Burnett Show*, gave Betty prime space to show her talents in the leaner years between *The Mary Tyler Moore Show* and *The Golden Girls*. A guest on Burnett's popular variety show just three times, Betty scored better with *Mama's Family* appearing in 15 original episodes (14 on NBC, one in syndication).

Originally brought to NBC in January 1983—CBS having taken a "pass" on a character and a show born on their network—*Mama's Family* was a mid-season replacement show and was built as a vehicle for Vicki Lawrence. Hungry for another hit and respectful of the franchise that created the show, NBC stuck with *Mama* and the rest of the Harper clan throughout the spring of 1983, and into the 1984-85 schedule. Its final *network* demise came in August 1985, ironically just as two of its characters (Betty and Rue McClanahan) were leaving the show as part of a launch of another *little* show on NBC—*The Golden Girls*.

But a mere cancelation by NBC could not stop Thelma Harper (played brilliantly by Burnett sidekick Lawrence). Oh no—*Mama's Family* came roaring back into first-run syndication in markets all across the country in September 1986—and lasted another four years as the most popular show in syndication at the time. (Did those network goons at NBC ever regret letting Mama go?)

Betty's part of *Mama's Family* was noteworthy. Her character, Mama's oldest and most spoiled child, Ellen Harper Jackson, was a terrific contrast to the low-brow Harper's. Ellen was a major social climber, trying desperately to get free from her humble Raytown roots to join the intelligencia of Raytown style and sophistication (if there is such a thing).

While the *Mama's Family* episodes airing on NBC (many of them directed by another Burnett colleague, the great Harvey Korman) had the same sometimes painful edge as the skits did on *The Carol Burnett Show*, once Mama moved into syndication *Mama's Family* grew more lovable and dare we say, gentler? The difference is perhaps best demonstrated by Mama's terminology for her only son, Vinton (played to aplomb by veteran TV actor Ken Berry): On the NBC version Mama would just call Vinton "a loser"—in syndication, she softened that to the funnier term, "lug nut."

Betty's character Ellen did everything to indicate she truly believed she was better than the rest of her kin—and Betty's sicky-sweet delivery was well-suited to the task. Lawrence's sharp-tongued Thelma was having none of it. She often cut Ellen down to size—but it was OK, Ellen could always turn on her sister Eunice (played in guest spots by the legendary Carol Burnett).

Particularly memorable episodes found the Harper family aware that Ellen was clueless about her husband Bruce's extra-marital affair with his secretary. It all works out as Ellen shows up next driving a brand-new Cadillac Seville.

Ed Higgins (played by Korman) asked, "Why, that is some machine! What did Bruce have to give up for that?"

Ellen smiles, "His secretary."

Ellen's marriage eventually fails as do her attempts at dating—especially a younger man. Mama, Vinton, Naomi (Dorothy Lyman) and Aunt Fran (Rue McClanahan) show up unexpectedly at Raytown's swankiest eatery, The Shea Ray, and surprise Ellen and her much-younger beau. Mama is not happy, and makes her unhappiness known, as always. The results are riotous but allow Betty and Vicki to play out a closing scene where the two bond (similar to cathartic healing moments between Mama and the Eunice character).

Ellen Harper also played a key role in a rare, two-part *Mama's Family* where Mama runs for and is elected Mayor of Raytown over Ellen's dear friend, Mayor Tutwiller (whom she affectionately calls "Tutty!"). Mayor Tutwiller also appears in a hilarious episode where Ellen is honored at the local country club as "Raytown's Woman of the Year"—an event Mama, Vinton and Naomi successfully ruin.

Betty's final appearance as the Ellen character (and the only one after the show went into syndication) was a riotous romp at Saint Ray Hospital when sister-in-law Naomi learns from one of her customers at the Food Circus that Ellen is hospitalized. Mama quickly grabs the whole family and drags them into Ellen's hospital room unannounced—saying she's there to "comfort my baby" but noting, "When I think of all the loved ones who have gone under the knife and died in this slap-happy meat market they call a hospital!"

Comforting Ellen proves difficult—a hungry grandson Bubba Higgins (played by Alan Kayser) has eaten all the chocolates bought for Ellen. Vinton has pulled up more weeds than flowers from Mama's garden to brighten her room, and Naomi brings along two discarded 1972 editions of *Readers' Digest* that she's grabbed off the toilet tank back at the Harper house. Between grabbing the rest of Ellen's hospital meal, arguing over the TV remote, and Mama threatening Bubba that if he doesn't shut up, "I'll skin your hide until hell won't have it!"—Ellen tosses her family out. Mama eventually learns why Ellen is in the hospital in the first place—she's having a "fanny tuck" to get her butt to "salute like it used to."

Mama and the rest of the Harper's would go on for another four years—but by then, Betty had taken up the biggest role of her career as Rose Nylund.

5

THE GOLDEN YEARS

NBC AND THE Girls STRIKE Gold

Going into the fall 1985 TV season, NBC executive Brandon Tartikoff found himself in an unusual position. Several of Tartikoff's underlings had openly criticized network rival CBS for its primetime lineup that continued to draw older and older viewers. Under Tartikoff, NBC had successfully roared back into the No. 1 position in the ratings with a stable of younger, more "hip" hit shows: *Cheers, The Cosby Show, Night Court, A Different World, Miami Vice, L.A. Law, Hill Street Blues,* and *St. Elsewhere.*

At the same time, however, NBC had also trotted out a new vehicle for TV gray-top veteran Andy Griffith in *Matlock,* and for '85 planned to launch an over-the-hill new sitcom: *The Golden Girls.*

Quickly compared to theatrical successes centering on stories of older characters such as *Cocoon* and *On Golden Pond,* Tartikoff and Co. were convinced despite the average age of the *Girls* cast being well into their 60s—that they had a sure-fire hit in their hands. They felt so strongly about it—they offered the show's creator Susan Harris a rare guarantee of 13 weeks—or a half season run—on NBC.

"*Golden Girls* defies all the demographic rules of television," said Tartikoff, while defending his decision to go forward with the show on the fall schedule.[150]

One of Tartikoff's top lieutenants, Warren Littlefield, at the time NBC's vice president for series development, was equally committed. "We knew the show would be breaking one of the basic television rules," Littlefield said. "But all of our best shows scared us a bit. We propelled *Golden Girls* because we knew there would be nothing like it on the air. And in the last year or two, what has worked on television is what is different."[151]

Tartikoff wasn't alone in his belief in the potential of *The Golden Girls*. Joel Segal, a Hollywood ad executive who viewed "up fronts" of the show declared that the show's pilot "mines laughs out of almost every line" and declared the show "outrageously funny."[152]

While hindsight has proven *The Golden Girls* to be one of TV's most successful, and most loved shows ever—in the summer of '85 the show represented risk. Beyond its older cast, the timeslot NBC selected for the show was thought by many to be certain death.

"In the 1980s, network TV on Saturday night has become a losing proposition, losing viewers to pay-cable movies, video cassette rentals and the networks' own inept programming," declared Fred Rothenberg, a TV writer for the Associated Press. "Saturday hasn't been funny since Mary Tyler Moore left Minneapolis and Bob Newhart surrendered his couch. But four 'golden girls' who don't play shuffleboard may beat the odds and put viewers back on the network couch."[153]

The viewers came back in droves. *The Golden Girls* premiere on September 14, 1985 was not only NBC's highest rated show of the week, it was the highest rated new show of the season overall.

New York Times Hollywood writer Aljean Harmetz noted TV had a love affair with female actors in comedy and drama—but they normally had one thing in common: youth. "Creamy skin and firm thighs are a prerequisite for leading roles," Harmetz wrote.[154]

Golden Girls creator Susan Harris noted, "A woman's worth is tied to what she looks like. At 82, Cary Grant could still be a romantic lead. But, on television, a woman over 50 is cast as an ax murderer."[155]

Harris described her work in creating *The Golden Girls* in almost the same terms as others describe a professional "calling."

"I had to write *Golden Girls*," Harris said. "I've never gotten excited about a network idea before, but this was compelling. I could write grown-ups. Television is always several steps behind life. When do you see passionate older people on television?"[156]

Harris said the show intended to break new ground—including showing older adults engaging in romantic adventures, storylines TV rarely displayed. Critics were quick to note that co-stars Bea Arthur and Rue McClanahan portrayed characters that were not that far from their own personalities and praised Betty for playing "against type" and welcomed Broadway veteran Estelle Getty's fresh take.

The enthusiasm expressed by Harris seemed to be shared by everyone else. Co-producer Paul Junger Witt declared the show's pilot was "perfect"—a rare accomplishment in network TV.

"When you're hoping that all the right talent comes together at just the right time, there's always an element of luck when you make a pilot, but we knew we had a great piece of material," Witt said. "Susan's script is widely considered one of the best pilots ever written. And thanks to our amazing cast, it turned out be one of the best pilots ever made."[157]

Betty and her *Golden Girls* co-stars (from left Estelle Getty, Rue McClanahan, and Beatrice Arthur) pose inside the Columbia-Sunset Gower Studios in Hollywood after taping a December 1985 episode. After 1987, the show was taped at Ren-Mar Studios in Hollywood. *(AP Photo/Nick Ut)*

Grant Tinker, then working his way up the food chain at NBC from his previous days with MTM Enterprises, said "We bought the *Golden Girls* based on the pilot, and it was a very funny show, but we didn't know it was going to be as popular as it was."[158]

Casting the Golden Girls

Selecting the cast of *The Golden Girls* reflects how important and valuable having just the right actor in each part can be. The result is TV magic—and among the most magical shows to come along in a long time was *The Golden Girls*.

The idea for the show started as a lark, according to author and TV writer Jim Colucci. Appearing at an "upfront" event for NBC, actresses Doris Roberts (then of NBC's *Remington Steele* and later on CBS' *Everybody Loves Raymond*) and Selma Diamond (of NBC's *Night Court*) stole the show as two outspoken, older ladies. The bit, given a working title of "Miami Nice" to play off NBC's unexpected big crime drama hit, *Miami Vice*, "Miami Nice" became the framework or outline for what would become *The Golden Girls*.

"Selma Diamond and I had great fun with the 'Miami Nice' bit," Roberts said. "We had a script, but we didn't have much time to rehearse, so we were sort of ad-libbing, too."[157]

NBC's Tartikoff was impressed nonetheless, telling Roberts he thought the bit had potential. Soon Tartikoff was asking Roberts how she felt about doing two shows at once—staying on *Remington Steele* as a supporting player, and helping launch what was still being called "Miami Nice."

Roberts was game for the idea, but had second thoughts , worried about stretching herself too thin to be effective in both places at once. Complicating matters was the unexpected death of Diamond on May 13, 1985.

But Tartikoff—revered among many in Hollywood for his commitment to ideas and his vision for new approaches—was not dissuaded. Interestingly, the network's 1984 smash hit, *The Cosby Show*, was part of the reason why.

Littlefield noted that *The Cosby Show* opened up a huge vein of talented black actors and actresses who struggled to gain a foothold in Hollywood film and TV. Casting Bill Cosby's hit show gave the producers, in essence, the cream of the crop. Tartikoff thought the same was true for older female actors—often shunted off to the side of the scene, or out of the production altogether—for their perceived lack of sex appeal. As a result, they knew a backlog of talented older female actresses were available to choose from.

NBC tapped into a trio of writers and producers who would soon become TV royalty- Susan Harris, Paul Junger Witt and Tony Thomas (who would later form Witt-Thomas-Harris Productions) to create 'Miami Nice' or whatever it was to become. Harris was deeply committed to the characters—*and* who should play them. From the start, she had envisioned "a Bea Arthur" type to play the character of Dorothy Zbornak.

Bea Arthur, however, wasn't interested. Even though she had read the script, and declared it good, she worried it was too much like her previous Maude Findlay character on her earlier CBS series, *Maude*. When she learned former *Maude* co-star Rue McClanahan was up for a part in the show, as was Betty White from *The Mary Tyler Moore Show*, Arthur declared she "wasn't interested in playing Maude and Vivian meet Sue Ann Nivens."

Discouraged that Arthur was not going to come on board, Harris relented and went along, reluctantly, with an NBC idea to bring in Broadway's lanky and sometimes cantankerous Elaine Stritch to read for the part of Dorothy. The reading went poorly— Stritch later working the rejection into her one-woman stage act.

Meanwhile, casting for the characters of Rose Nylund and Blanche Devereaux moved forward—but not as one might think. Both Betty and McClanahan were told that the Blanche character was built for Betty White. McClanahan coveted the role, but agreed to read for the Rose character regardless.

After doing so, the show's director Jay Sandrich asked both women to switch roles. It was soon apparent, McClanahan was meant to play Blanche—and Betty, playing against her previous Sue Ann type, was brilliant as Rose.

"As an actor, you get so many bad scripts, but when I read the pilot script for *The Golden Girls*, I sat up and took notice," Betty said. "It was different from anything I'd gotten. And it was all because of the wonderful writing."[160]

Betty notes that "as an actor, you can screw up a good show, but you can't save a bad one if it's not on the page."[161]

By now the name *Golden Girls* had replaced 'Miami Nice,' but the role of Dorothy remained uncast. McClanahan, based on her experience with Arthur on *Maude*, was recruited to make another entreaty to Arthur. It was worth the effort—once Arthur learned who would play Rose and Blanche—she relented and joined the cast.

"The next thing you know, the four of us came into read for the suits at NBC, and we laid them low. And that's the way they cast it," McClanahan recalled.[162]

One of the show's original characters—a gay housekeeper and cook named Coco (played by actor Charles Levin)—appears only in the show's pilot episode. Producers were so impressed with how the four *ladies* on the show interacted, a tough choice was made and the character Coco was out, and Estelle Getty's role as Sophia was increased dramatically.

Betty said from the very first "table read" of the pilot script—where the actors sit around the table and read through their lines in order—"we knew we were on to something. Everyone was so perfectly cast that the minute you heard the lines coming out of our mouths, it was exciting. I've never had a read-through like that."[163]

Appearing on the December 1986 *Barbara Walters Special* on ABC, Betty shared Walters' surprise that a show about four senior women could draw an audience of 35 million viewers, and crack the ratings top 10. Part of the success, she said, was the relevancy of the characters.

For example, "The girls are all still sexually interested, but they're not promiscuous. I think promiscuity is wrong regardless of your age, but they're still sexually interested and interesting. We've been very open and frank about sex on the show," Betty said.[164]

Betty said the show's characters don't necessarily reflect the personalities of the actresses who play them—noting that both she and Bea Arthur are shy in their personal lives. And Betty doesn't covet sharing her senior years with three friends—"I don't mind being alone, I like being alone. I am alone, as opposed to being lonely."[165]

Not everyone feels the same, Betty acknowledges. "I know for some people, being alone would the nightmare of the world. My husband Allen, couldn't think of being alone. If I was out of town for two nights, he would plan to eat dinner with someone because he couldn't think of being alone."[166]

Getting to Know Rose Nylund

"It is Betty White who is playing furthest from her real persona as Rose, who makes an art of naiveté," wrote *The New York Times'* Aljean Harmetz.[167]

Betty told reporters her natural instinct is "to smart off" but she knows the character of Rose Nylund wouldn't know a smart remark—even the ones aimed at her.

But Betty acknowledged that some of Rose's life—and her lines on the show—run painfully parallel to he own life. "A couple of speeches Rose makes get me by the throat," Betty said. "All I have to do is substitute 'Allen' for (the name) 'Charlie,' Rose's husband."[168]

"There's a lot more to Rose in me than I ever dreamed of," Betty said. "The only difference is that Rose was born in Minnesota and I was born in Oak Park, Illinois. I'm finding more 'Bettyisms' in Rose: Scary sometimes, but fun."[169]

Betty always defended her character Rose as not being an idiot, but rather "a complete innocent. She takes every word for its exact, literal meaning."[170]

Pointing out several scripts where the character of Rose gets to show her frighteningly serious competitive streak, Betty believes this is further evidence she's not an idiot. "When it comes to sports, this wimpy person suddenly turns into a tigress!" Betty said.[171]

The softer character of Rose wasn't relegated to the second level, or B-story line in every episode either. In one important episode of the fifth season called "72 Hours," Rose is notified that a blood transfusion she received during an earlier surgery may have been contaminated with HIV, the virus that causes AIDS. During the show, Rose must wait 72 hours to learn the results of her HIV test—providing an interesting opportunity for Rose and Blanche to bond, and for Rose to expand her world view.

"Of all the characters, (the writers) selected Rose, the most unlikely one really, to confront the issue of HIV," Betty said. "And seeing her panic but in the same way, in a comedic way, but not making fun of the subject at all."[172]

White added, "Not only were people understandably afraid of AIDS, but a lot of people wouldn't even admit it existed. So this was a daring episode to do, and the writers went straight for it."[173]

Picking Rose as the character to deal with an AIDS scare was an interesting choice, White believed. Blanche's character "was such a busy lady, but if it had been her story it would have taken on a whole other color. But with Rose being Miss Not-Always-With-It, it came as a real surprise. And I know it sounds corny to say, but I'm proud there was a little learning in this episode. I think the audience went away knowing a little more about the subject than they knew going in."[174]

The show's writers and producers also placed Betty's character in an unexpected spot during *The Golden Girls'* second season in an episode titled, "Isn't It Romantic?" Dorothy's gay friend Jean (played by veteran actor Lois Nettleton) comes to visit and subsequently develops romantic feelings for Rose. Perhaps most remembered for an incredibly funny scene in which McClanahan's character Blanche mistakes the word "lesbian" for "Lebanese," the script reveals more depth to Rose than viewers may have expected.

"Even someone as naïve as Rose is able to sense when something is outside her ordinary realm of experience, and so she senses that Jean is attracted to her," Betty said. "The writers gave me that lovely speech where I talk to her in the kitchen, and I loved that they weren't afraid to cross boundaries and go to places like that."[175]

The show won heavy ratings and critical acclaim—McClanahan earning her 1987 Emmy award for that show, and Nettleton winning a guest spot Emmy nomination (but not winning the trophy).

Rose's character was the only *Golden Girl* with a steady beau (prior to the two-part final episodes of the series when Dorothy gets engaged and married to Blanche's uncle Lucas, played by Leslie Nielsen). Her love—college professor Miles Webber—appeared for three seasons. "That's a long-term relationship in TV terms," Betty said. "Miles was played by a very lovely actor, Harold Gould as Miles and Rose edged toward marriage."[176]

Sadly, though, the Rose-Miles love affair was eventually doomed, as revealed in a surprising episode of *The Golden Palace*, the CBS spin-off in the year after *The Golden Girls* ended its run on NBC. Miles discloses that he's fallen in love with another woman and is not sure how to choose between Rose and the other woman.

How did Betty compare being on *The Golden Girls* to her earlier run on *The Mary Tyler Moore Show*?

"(Mary's show) was the happiest experience ever until *The Golden Girls*. The only thing that makes *The Golden Girls* better is I can be on every week. The most I ever did in a season was 12 (episodes) with Mary," Betty said.

She again credits the show's writers. "The magic of the show was the way the writers drew our characters so distinctly," she said.

Off-screen, celebrity tabloids pressed a lot of ink suggesting there was tension between the four *Golden Girls*, but that couldn't be more untrue, Betty said. The only tension on the set, Betty said, was when she'd goof around on the set and that "Bea (Arthur) put up with it just so long, and she let you have just so much string, and then all of a sudden, when she'd had enough, she just lets out with 'Please!' And I shape up fast!"[177]

Betty was asked recently what she thinks what her character Rose Nylund would be doing today. She's convinced Rose "would just sort of retire and not be the sharpest knife in the drawer, but I think she'd still be having a good time. Anybody who thinks that Bob Hope was her father is not the brightest you've ever seen."[178]

Rose-Centered Episodes

With a foursome to write for, the writers of *The Golden Girls* had plenty of storylines to work with. As with most situation comedies, *The Golden Girls* relied on a main or "A" story line to carry each episode, with a secondary or "B" story line added in for transitions and comic relief. As is the case with many classic shows, sometimes the "B" story line steals the show and produces some of the most memorable moments.

Betty was blessed to be at the center of most of the action on the show—and the center of many story lines. Writer Marc Cherry noted once that he and other writers on the show would make a conscious effort to move the stories around so that each actress would have her moment to shine.

Betty's moments came—it seems—in both "A" and "B" story lines, and viewers ate it up, making the lovable nature of her character Rose Nylund clearly the very sweetest of the "girls." Several notable episodes featured Rose's story, including:

 ## SEASON 1

Rose the Prude—Originally broadcast September 28, 1985

Rose is bored with the men she's been meeting and considers giving up dating. "I'm tired of going out and not enjoying myself," she says. "All the men I meet act so old. Last week I went out with this man who talked for two hours about his prostate problems. I lived in Minnesota for 51 years and I never even heard of a prostate!" Regardless, Rose agrees to a fix-up date Blanche sets up for her. Rose and her new friend hit it off so well, he invites her away for the weekend. Her new love interest—Arnie Peterson—is played by actor Harold Gould who is cast in later episodes as Rose's steady beau, Miles Webber. Rose wants to go on the outing—but she has fear too—turns out her husband Charlie died in bed in the throws of lovemaking. "I haven't been with a man in that special way since Charlie died," Rose confesses. "It's true. Charlie was the only lover I ever had and my first time was on our wedding night. Maybe it sounds strange, but without Charlie I thought that part of my life was over, I never gave it a second thought." Rose's doubts are based on the idea she would be unfaithful to Charlie, even though she hasn't been with another man in the 15 years since he died. "I'm afraid that if I make love to you, I may kill you," Rose blurts out. Arnie deadpans, "Well, if you haven't made love in 15 years, that's a possibility!" In the end, Rose shares her bed with Arnie and declares, "Being with Arnie made me realize I can be with a man again without feeling guilty about it. Oh, it's a nice feeling that when one part of your life is over, another part can begin."

The Competition—Originally broadcast November 2, 1985

Here we learn of Rose's over-the-top competitive nature where she continually manipulates her bowling partner to get any advantage she can in a women's doubles bowling tournament. She admits, "I admit it, I have a problem. I'm too competitive when it comes to athletics." Finally convincing Dorothy to be her partner, Rose adds, "Just say yes, Dorothy and no one will get hurt . . . unless we lose."

During the competition, Rose's behavior is terrible—calling Sophia "Ma" just to get under Dorothy's skin, and donning a replica of Blanche's beloved satin bowling shirt: "Don't worry Blanche, no one will notice (we're wearing the same top), it looks so different on a woman with a full bosom."

Break In—Originally broadcast November 9, 1985
Rose is overcome with fear after a burglary that occurs while the girls are out attending a Madonna concert. First a guard dog, then a burglar alarm, even a hand-held spray bottle of mace (that Blanche mistakenly thinks is hair spray and ends up macing herself in the face) can't assuage Rose's fear. Finally, Rose buys a gun and accidently "kills" Blanche's prized Chinese vase when she thinks she hears a prowler. Sophia notes, "I managed to live 80, 81 years. I survived pneumonia, two operations, a stroke. One night I'll belch and Stable Mable here will blow my head off!" Rose finally overcomes her fear by fighting back against a man she thinks is a purse snatcher—"I dropped him like a sack of potatoes" by "kneeing him in his safe deposit box!" Turns out the 'attacker' was the parking lot attendant trying to give Rose her keys back—who apparently has agreed not to sue Rose.

A Little Romance—Originally broadcast December 14, 1985
Rose is dating one of the counselors at the Grief Center where she works, Dr. Jonathan Newman (played by Brent Newman). "Rose is dating a psychiatrist? It's about time!" Sophia declares. Rose's reluctance to invite him over (and reveal that he is a small person) causes Blanche to step in an invite to dinner without Rose's knowledge. A hilarious stream of mis-steps and mis-speaks follows as Dorothy (and especially) Blanche try to ignore that Dr. Newman stands only waist high. Dorothy asks if she can take Dr. Newman's "height"—when she means hat. Even the menu for the night is potentially insulting—shrimp as an appetizer and short ribs for the entre. Blanche seems to stumble over one short-man remark after another, even declaring, "It really is a small world." Dr. Newman overlooks all the oafish behavior

and expresses his attraction for Rose—but still breaks it off—because Rose is not Jewish. Noted small person actor Billy Barty and "psychic to the stars" Jeanne Dixon make guest appearances in Rose's dream sequence.

In a Bed of Rose's—Originally broadcast January 11, 1986
Rose finally relents to pressure from the man she's dating and lets him spend the night. Tragedy strikes again—as her male friend dies in his sleep during the night—just as her belated husband Charlie did 15 years earlier. "Oh Sophia, he's not dead, he's shy," Rose says, trying to reassure herself that history is not repeating itself. Sophia responds, "He's dead I tell you, it's gonna be 98 degrees today. Let a dead guy lay in your bed, it won't be pretty. You could light a firecracker off in his nostrils and you won't wake him!" In trying to notify his family, Rose learns her beau is actually a married man and she's just his latest fling. Rose breaks the news of his death to his wife and Rose begins to vow she'll never sleep with another man again, but relents and sees a new guy.

Job Hunting—Originally broadcast March 8, 1986
Blanche is on a diet, but the really bad news is that Rose is losing her job because the grief center is closing. As you might expect, though, Rose is more concerned about all the people who count on the center for grief counseling, to the point of not being able to get on with the task of finding a new job. Rose notes what she's got going for her in getting a new job: "I'm dependable, friendly, loyal, eager!" Dorothy adds, "That's great. If she can learn to catch a Frisbee in her teeth she can find work as a golden retriever!" Dorothy and Blanche eventually have to confront Rose about all the time she's spending on her former clients from the center, instead of finding a job. Rose reveals she has had job interviews, but has had no luck, mostly because of her age. "I never think of myself as too old, but everyone else does! Maybe I am old, old and useless! And terrified!" All of the girls' crisis converge around the kitchen table for one of the first of many

confabs over a cheesecake (and cookies 'n cream ice cream, and Oreo cookies, and whatever else was in the cupboard). The conversation, as usual, turns to a discussion of sex, and their very first sexual experiences. Rose reveals Charlie was her first lover—on her wedding night. "I had never seen a man before," Rose says. "The only things I ever saw were the animals on the farm, you know, the bulls and the horses." (Blanche noting that they must have been a tough act for Charlie to follow!) Rose adds "that first night, I was kind of appalled, I guess." She adds that "it was five years before I knew what made your eyes roll back in your head!" Blanche offers she couldn't wait until she was married. "People in the south mature faster. I think it's the heat." Dorothy adds, "I think it's the gin."

Blind Ambitions—Originally broadcast Mach 29, 1986
Rose's newly-blind sister Lily (played by actress Polly Holliday) comes to visit—but only to convince Rose to go back to Chicago with her to take care of her. Lily claims she's independent, but privately is begging Rose for help. Rose is conflicted, but decides not to go to Chicago, instead encouraging Lily to try and learn to do for herself and avoid a hopeless life. Lily leaves while angrily vowing never to bother Rose again. During Lily's visit, the girls put together an ill-fated garage sale causing Rose to ask: "Could we get in trouble having a garage sale? I mean, after all, we're not actually selling a garage!" Sophia advises Dorothy and Blanche that if it comes down to Rose or her sister Lily needing to make change for their garage sale customers, "let the blind one do it!" Lily eventually goes home, back to a blind school, and invites Rose to visit to demonstrate how she has gained her independence back. "Oh Rose, I had to see you again because I felt terrible about how we left things," Lilly offers. "Rose, I owe you an apology. I was angry at the world because I couldn't see it anymore. That's why I wanted you to take care of me, but you didn't give me any choice. I needed you to *see* that you were right!"

 SEASON 2

Ladies of the Evening—Originally broadcast October 4, 1986
The house has to be fumigated and Blanche has won three tickets to see Burt Reynolds in a Miami dinner-theatre production and after-party. Even though Sophia can't go, the four girls plan a weekend at a Miami Beach hotel, but trouble is not far behind. Blanche had picked the hotel, not for its location or price, but because it was the one with the most men hanging out in the lobby! Turns out the guys are there for a reason—the hotel is a front for a brothel. A police raid ensues and the girls are swept up with the prostitutes on site, and get booked in jail. In jail, the girls lament not only missing a chance encounter with Burt Reynolds, but also the nastiness of being locked up "with all this common gutter trash," as Blanche refers to the other women present. Her remarks almost start a cell riot, until Dorothy steps in and breaks it up—declaring that breaking up a cell fight isn't much different than her work in the public schools. Rose is perhaps most depressed, declaring missing a chance to meet Burt is a bigger disappointment than losing the Miss Butter Queen Contest back in St. Olaf. "From the time I was born I was groomed for the contest . . . for 16 years my entire life revolved around butter!" Rose declares. She recalls the big night that she thought the Butter Queen crown would finally be hers—she had done well in the question and answer round, even avoiding being tripped up by a trick margarine question. "That evening, butter was spelled R-O-S-E!" Determined to rid herself of her "bitter butter memories," Rose details the pageant's grand finale that apparently involved—gasp!—butter churn tampering.

It's a Miserable Life—Originally broadcast November 1, 1986
Rose tries everything to convince grouchy neighbor Frieda Claxton (played to aplomb by actress Nan Martin) to stop the city from cutting down a 200-year-old tree on her property. Everyone but Rose thinks it's because Mrs. Claxton is a horrible person—"Half the kids in the neighborhood last year wore Frieda Claxton costumes for Halloween!" Dorothy

declares. Rose isn't convinced and tries to win over Frieda with some home-made Danish rolls. It doesn't work—Frieda is only nice just to get the Danish—particularly the prune ones! Fed up, Rose finally tells Frieda to "shut up and let us have our say" and adds, "And if you don't like it, you can just sit there and shut up or drop dead!" Shockingly, that's just what Frieda does, and Rose is convinced she's killed the old bird. Rose is overcome with grief and guilt, thinking she killed the woman—and the girls make a hilarious trip to the funeral home to pay for Mrs. Claxton's funeral. Dorothy promptly informs the funeral director that "we're bereaved on a budget." No one shows for Mrs. Claxton's last rites, providing she really did have no one who cared about her. Rose makes herself feel better after spreading Mrs. Claxton's ashes at the base of the big tree, causing the city to abandon plans to cut it down for a road widening project.

Isn't It Romantic?—Originally broadcast November 8, 1986
This episode won riotous laughs, *and* Emmy awards for the show as Dorothy's high school friend Jean visits. Jean (played by actress Lois Nettleton) is just getting over the death of her lesbian partner, and thinks she's falling in love with Rose (who Dorothy hasn't told about Jean's sexual orientation). While Dorothy and Sophia find humor in Jean's crush on Rose, Blanche is at first confused about the difference between a lesbian and a Lebanese person. Once she gets it, her confusion turns to insult when she learns that Jean prefers Rose over her: "To think Jean would prefer Rose over me, that's ridiculous! Now you tell me the truth, if you had to pick between me and Rose, who would you choose!?" Jean eventually confesses her emerging feelings for Rose—and naïve, innocent Rose finally gets it. "You only said what you were feeling," Rose said. "I have to admit, I don't understand these kinds of feelings, but if I did understand, and if I were like you, I think I would be very flattered and proud that you thought of me that way . . . you don't have to go unless you think our friendship alone is not enough." It is enough, and Rose and Jean remain friends.

Family Affair—Originally broadcast November 22, 1986
Rose's daughter Bridget (played by Marilyn Jones) is visiting at the same time Dorothy's gad-fly son Michael (actor Scott Jacoby) is in town. The two kids end up in bed, making no one happy. A fight ensues between Rose and Dorothy after Rose implies that Michael is not good enough for her daughter. Rose has some growing to do—she thought naively that her daughter was still a virgin. She's not. "I've never seen Bridget in bed with a man before, unless you count Raggedy Andy!" The truth out in the open, Rose's daughter wants to talk about adult topics, prompting Rose's reply, "Can't we just get matching mother daughter outfits instead?"

Love, Rose—Originally broadcast December 13, 1986
While in the midst of a dating drought, Dorothy and Blanche convince Rose to place a personal ad. Blanche pursues the point: "Rose, have you ever considered advertising?" Rose gets in an unexpected jab with, "Oh Blanche! I could never dress the way you do! Besides, I have to wear undies. Not all of my wool skirts are lined." Rose finally decides to place a personal ad, but the dating woes grow as no one replies. No one until Blanche enlists Dorothy's help in forging up a reply from none other than a man named "Isaac Q. Newton" (played by actor Paul Dooley). Torrid letters are exchanged, and Rose wants to meet Isaac—finding him listed in the phone book. As expected, Rose is embarrassed and heartbroken when she learns it was all a lie. "The worst part was making me think that somebody felt those special things about me," Rose says. "Somebody who wanted to hear why sometimes I hate my job, or why I sometimes eat my lunch alone in the park. It was so important to me that someone actually listened to me, someone actually cared about me as much as the person who wrote those letters. It meant so much to me to have someone like that in my life." Realizing it was Blanche and Dorothy who wrote the letters—and it is *they* who love and care for Rose, even her stories—she decides to forgive the girls.

Before and After—Originally broadcast January 24, 1987

Rose is overdoing it, volunteering for almost everything in town, and suffers the first of several health challenges—this time a close call from an esophageal spasm. Blanche is excited after meeting Rose's doctor, Dr. Wallerstein. "Oh Dorothy, she's gonna be alright, her doctor's a Jew!" Rose is convinced she's undergone a near-death experience, and believes she's not living life to the fullest. As a result, she finds some new "beach" friends to run with—and even moves out of Blanche's house to live closer to the ocean. All is not well, though. Her new roommates don't have time for each other—it's nothing like living with Blanche, Dorothy and Sophia. Feeling lonely and ignored, Rose sneaks back home to see if the girls will take her back, suggesting to the bored ladies: "We could do what we normally do, talk dirty and pig out." That sounds right to everyone—and the show ends with the ladies back where they started, around a cheesecake on the kitchen table.

Bedtime Story—Originally aired February 7, 1987

The girls recall times when they've had to double-up and share beds because of house guests. Through flashbacks, a series of scenarios are set up—including the four girls crammed into Sophia's bed during a cold night with a broken furnace. Rose makes everyone miserable with her bunny-nose slippers and long-winded prayers—answered, she thinks, by the voice of God (which is actually Dorothy). Dorothy assures Rose that God wouldn't mind if she skipped her prayers for one night, "He's very busy these days. Most of his free time is spent talking to Pat Robertson!" Rose's prayers are sincere: She thinks God is doing a terrific job, "although there are some things I don't understand like poverty and the spokesmodel category on *Star Search*." As the girls reminisce, it's another reminder that Rose's cooking isn't the hit of the house—Sophia declaring that the girls don't want to eat Rose's chipped beef because it will "test their gag reflex." Another memory reignites Rose's fear of thunderstorms at night and her childhood memories of the "St. Olaf Slasher—"he terrorized St. Olaf for months. In the dark of night, he'd sneak into an unsuspecting farmer's field and mercilessly slash his scarecrow to shreds! He was also suspected in the disfigurement of several whisk brooms!"

A Piece of Cake—Originally broadcast May 9, 1987
Another flashback episode where the girls recall birthdays past starts off with a bang as Rose's balloon animal, "Scottie" is promptly popped by Dorothy. Rose recalls her last birthday in St. Olaf, Minnesota before moving to Miami. Her beloved Charlie has passed and she's made the tough choice to move on, the old family house in Minnesota carrying too many memories to allow her to move on. Although alone, Rose bakes a cake for herself so she can have a heart-to-heart talk with her departed husband. "This is the first special day I've had to spend without you, Charlie," Rose says. "I just wanted you to know what I had decided. I hope to be in Florida before the next winter comes, but I know wherever I am, you will be right there with me. I love you Charlie! I miss you!" Dorothy's memory is more of a horror story—as Rose signs her up as the grouchiest (and oldest) "birthday round-up" special guest at Mr. Ha Ha's Hot Dog Hacienda.

 SEASON 3

Old Friends—Originally broadcast September 19, 1987
The third season opener has a story focused on Sophia's new friend with Alzheimer's. The "B" story line features Rose and Blanche helping out a local "Sunshine Cadet" troop—and Blanche mistakenly giving Rose's prized teddy bear, Fernando, to one of the girls. The little girl Daisy (played by Jenny Lewis), is no girl scout. She holds Rose's bear for ransom, even cutting off and sending Blanche one of his fuzzy ears to make her point. Eventually Rose takes matters into her own hands—literally—noting, "I've been doing a lot thinking. If after all the years of love and companionship, Fernando and I are meant to part company, I'll just have to accept that. From time to time, life deals you an unfriendly hand. There's nothing you can do about it. I guess there's a

lesson to be learned here." With that, Rose rips Fernando from Daisy's hands and shoves the little girl out the door. "Sometimes life just isn't fair, kiddo!"

One for the Money—Originally broadcast September 26, 1987
One of several "flashback" shows in which the girls recall earlier times—this time we get to see the charity dance marathon that all three girls want to win. We also get to see Rose's dancing skills—"They didn't call me the 'dancin' fool' for nothing!" she gloats. Dorothy asks, "Oh yeah, and when did they drop the dancin' part?" Rose wows 'em all by doing back flips and the splits—all done by a stunt double wearing a wig and dress to match Rose. It doesn't matter, it's a hilarious glimpse once again into the terribly competitive side of Rose Nylund.

Bringing up Baby—Originally broadcast October 3, 1987
Rose's uncle Hickenblotter has died back in Minnesota, and has left his "baby" to Rose. Turns out "baby" is a full-grown pig, a five-time best pig winner at the Minnesota State Fair, which comes with a $100,000 caretakers' allowance. "If we give this baby love and attention and understanding, it will turn out fine," Rose declares. Blanche and Dorothy go along with the scheme after learning "Baby" is 29-years-old—four more than the expected lifespan of a pig. "Baby" is not well, and Rose even wants to take his temperature, "Although I don't even know what a normal temperature is for a pig." Sophia adds, "I know a ham turns out nicely at 325 degrees." Guilt gets the best of the group, though, and "Baby" is sent back to Minnesota to live with Rose's cousin Gunther. Days later, "Baby" dies and Gunther collects all the money.

Letter to Gorbachev—Originally broadcast October 31, 1987
Rose's naivety strikes again, this time a letter she's written letters to President Ronald Reagan and Soviet Premier Mikhail Gorbachev about the risk of nuclear war. Rose's letter is mistaken as coming from a nine-year-old girl in

Rose's Sunshine Cadets troop. Rose's childhood worries weren't about nuclear war, but about important topics like whether she'd ever been crowned St. Olaf's "Small Curd Cottage Cheese Queen"—the town's second-highest honor (right after "Large Curd Cottage Cheese Queen"). Rose is embarrassed to learn the Soviet's don't know her political views were those of an adult. Her letter reveals great sincerity about reducing the threat of nuclear weapons— and even moves the Gorbachev's Soviet ambassador to announce he's defecting!

Three on a Couch—Originally broadcast December 5, 1987
Yet another flashback episode set-up by an emergency visit by the girls to a psychiatrist (played by Philip Sterling) to help them resolve their seemingly insurmountable differences. Rose's biggest complaint is the girls are always telling her to shut up—and perhaps for good reason. Dorothy recalls Rose mistakenly placing her classified ad, "Willing to do anything, $8 an hour" in the personals column. The guys who show up have some very special "work" on their mind for Dorothy to complete. As Blanche notes, "The point is Rose, you're doing something stupid all of the time. And if you're not doing something stupid, or saying something stupid, or wearing something stupid, you're cooking something stupid." Rose is insulted and calls Blanche one of her favorite Swedish put-downs— a "gerconanococken"—roughly translated to being equal to dog poop that's turned white. She even tells Dorothy to "blow it out your toobenburbles!" Even though the psychiatrist has declared the girls as incompatible and unable to live together—they decide (surprise!) to stay together anyway!

Charlie's Buddy—Originally broadcast December 15, 1987
Rose receives an unexpected visitor, Buddy Rourke (played by Milo O'Shea) who claims to be one of Charlie Nylund's Army buddies from 43 years ago. "Charlie Nylund was one of finest men I ever met," Buddy tells Rose. "I realized that a whole lifetime had passed, and I had never laid eyes on

my old buddy's favorite gal." Buddy conjures up all sorts of old memories from Rose's past with Charlie, though it's all a set up for his plan to trick Rose into signing over her money. Buddy's plan to have Rose live with him without the benefit of marriage prompts a spirited argument among the girls. "I'm comfortable with Buddy, it's easier being with him because he already knows so much about me," Rose confides, though it's not clear she truly loves Buddy. Rose decides not to go with Buddy, just as a sudden flash of conscience overcomes Buddy and he moves on—deciding not to dupe Rose out of her money.

Mister Terrific—Originally broadcast April 30, 1988
Rose has a new love interest, children's TV show host "Mr. Terrific" who wears a costume startlingly similar to Superman. Mr. Terrific, played by Bob Dishy, meets Rose at a mall where he was signing autographs. "Girls, you won't believe what happened to me this afternoon," Rose declares, "I met Mr. Terrific!" Blanche cautions, "I once thought I had met Mr. Terrific. Turns out there was also a Mrs. Terrific. I found myself ducking a Mr. Vase!" Rose gets Dorothy a job as an educational consultant for "Mr. Terrific's Clubhouse" but after a run-in with his producer and with the help of newly-hired Dorothy, Mr. Terrific becomes Mr. Unemployed. With Rose's help, Mr. Terrific gets his job back and everything works out.

Mother's Day—Originally broadcast May 7, 1988
The girls spend time remembering Mother's Day moments from the past. Rose's flashback includes being stuck in a bus station en route to St. Olaf to visit her kids. "My children figured it would be cheaper if I came here to visit them, instead of all of them coming to see me," Rose says. The woman she meets (Geraldine Fitzgerald) asks, "They figured that out, all by themselves? And they live in St. Olaf?" The same woman knows about St. Olaf—a city of beautiful streets and charming homes—"all filled with idiots." Rose is not insulted, acknowledging that per capita, the level of

idiocy in St. Olaf is above-average. Rose eventually claims the woman as her mother to help her avoid being picked up by the police for being AWOL from the nursing home.

SEASON 4

Yokel Hero—Originally broadcast November 5, 1988
Blanche and Dorothy make an ill-advised decision that gets Rose named "St. Olaf's Woman of the Year"—as confirmed by Len, Sven and Ben, triplets sent from Minnesota to confirm the winner—"Oooompa!" Seems the girls have pumped Rose's application full of lies, betraying her trust much like they did earlier in their attempts to help her get a date via the personal ads. Once again, Rose forgives the girls. "I thought it all over, and you were just trying to help me and I can't stay mad at my best friends," Rose says. "After all, we've eaten over 500 cheesecakes together. Besides you weren't raised in St. Olaf. It is not your fault that you're chronic, two-faced liars!"

Scared Straight—Originally broadcast December 10, 1988
Blanche's unmarried brother Clayton (actor Monte Markham) pays a visit—and can't bring himself to tell his sister that he's gay. He does confide in Rose, but also decides to lie and tell Blanche that he and Rose slept together. Blanche is not happy—calling Rose a "cradle-snatching, two-faced, empty-headed dummy" They are words Blanche will have to eat and she'll have to ask Rose for forgiveness when Clayton finally tells the truth—but not before Sophia declares him to be "as gay as a picnic basket." Blanche says, "There's something I have to say to you, Rose honey. It's just too little words, but they're the hardest two little words in all the world for me to say." Rose replies, "What, 'not tonight'?" Everything works out—with Rose telling Blanche she is just happy "that you thought to say 'I'm sorry' considering what a selfish, conceited person you are."

The Impotence of Being Earnest—Originally broadcast Feb. 4, 1989
Rose's newest love interest has a bit of a problem—he's impotent. Ernie, played by Richard Herd, is a divorced corporate attorney and looking to date again. Rose is dismayed that after a month of dating, Ernie hasn't even tried to put the moves on her. She thought he might have been once, but "it turns out he was just looking for his napkin under the table." Eventually Ernie asks Rose away for a romantic weekend, but has to confess his sexual impotency. Rose understands, tosses her drink over her shoulder (the romantic times over) and suggests, "Why don't we see what's playing at the movies!" Rose steps in it a bit over dinner when she remarks about her soufflé—"there's nothing more frustrating than waiting for one of these suckers to rise and they just won't!" but quickly adds, "That's no reflection on you Ernie." Rose's patience pays off—and Ernie overcomes his problem—so much so, he decides to dump Rose to go back to his wife. Worried that she's heartbroken by getting dumped, Dorothy and Blanche try to console Rose. "Now don't you be upset, Rose," Blanche says. "You gave him back his manhood." Rose gets the last laugh with, "If he can find it, he can have it! He's probably the worst lover I've ever had!"

Valentine's Day—Originally broadcast February 11, 1989
Another "flashback" show where the girls remember Valentine's Day celebrations gone by. The girls are still trying to forgive Rose for the time she booked them at a clothing-optional mountain retreat. Rose didn't read the brochure—she just liked the pictures. The girls decide to try and go along with the crowd and go down to dinner naked—after finally shedding bed sheets and large, heart-shaped signs from the hotel lobby. Trouble is—they're the only ones naked in the dining room. The maitre d is having none of it: "Excuse me ladies, but we always *dress* for dinner here. And in your case, we'd appreciate it if you would do that for all three meals."

You Gotta Have Hope—Originally broadcast February 25, 1989
Dorothy is chairwoman of a benefit talent show. Sophia can't be in the show, but she introduces the "Donatello Triplets"—which are actually Eadie, Elena and Milly Del Rubio—the Del Rubio Triplets. Rose offers to help by getting Bob Hope as the emcee of the show claiming he's her father! "I'm serious Bob Hope is my father, well, sort of, he could be," she says. An orphan for the first eight years of her life, Rose confesses that she daydreamed that her real father was Bob Hope. "Believing he was my father got me through some really tough times," she said. "All my life I felt as if he was there if I needed him, so I know he won't let me down now." Rose's hopes aren't reality, though, and even a scheme to intercept him at a local golf club (complete with the girls donning men's golfing clothes) falls short. She eventually has to face reality –that her fantasies about Bob Hope aren't reality. Sophia saves the day, however, as Hope is the former Vaudevillian partner of her friend, and shows up at the last minute to save the show!

Little Sister—Originally broadcast April 1, 1989
Rose's younger sister Holly (played by actress Inge Svenson) shows up for a visit. Rose is not happy—seems Holly always has a way of stealing Rose's friends, all the fun, and this time, Blanche's boyfriend. Holly even tells versions of St. Olaf stories that Blanche and Dorothy *actually enjoy!* Rose is convinced Holly is leaving her out of the fun on purpose—but the girls don't agree. Eventually, it's revealed Rose's instincts are correct—Holly *is* being cruel. Rose tells her sister, "You walk in here, borrow my friends for awhile, start acting like a stupid jerk, and then waltz out like nothing has happened." Turns out Holly is jealous of Rose. "I used to feel so guilty for not getting along with you, but that's over now. Just because we're sisters doesn't mean we have to be friends; I'd like to be someday. But you're going to have to make the first move."

 **SEASON 5**

Rose Fights Back—Originally broadcast October 21, 1989
Rose gets bad news in a letter—and no, it wasn't a trick move by her "checkers-by-mail" partner—it's news that Charlie's pension checks won't be coming anymore. Rose goes looking for a better paying job, but struggles to find one—most places telling her she's too old. She seeks out the help of local TV consumer reporter Enrique Mas (played by actor Chick Vennera). Rose eventually lands the job as Mas' production assistant—but not until she makes the girls test out various products for the show including some painful methods to remove leg hair. "I know, let's just all set each other on fire instead," Dorothy deadpans. Rose also tests out inflatable pants meant to suck the fat from your legs. Sophia asks, "Does it come in a hat?"

Great Expectations—Originally broadcast January 13, 1990
Rose joins a group focused on positive thinking. Though they declare everyone in the room, it seems, as "Special!" they won't say it to Rose. Despite that, she declares "Life is so terrific! I feel like life is one big, giant weenie roast, and I'm the biggest weenie!" Rose does convince negatively driven Dorothy to come to a meeting (and Sophia comes along under the fake name of "Melanie Griffith"). When Rose tells Sophia, "After all, today is the first day of the rest of your life!" Sophia replies, "Terrific. If I'm lucky I may live to be seven!" The positive thinking concepts are rather basic—but Rose struggles to understand.

All Bets Are Off—Originally broadcast April 28, 1990
Rose's amateur paintings catch the eye of one of the big shots at the museum where Blanche works. She's painted the spring, winter and summer of St. Olaf—but can't paint "the fall of St. Olaf," because as Rose puts it, "it hasn't happened yet." One of the horses in Rose's painting is Old Brisker who "incidentally because of a printing error on the ballot was

elected water commissioner of St. Olaf for six months." Meanwhile, Dorothy's gambling problem resurfaces and Rose agrees to loan her an ATM card so she can get more money. That's the final straw—and Dorothy's guilt breaks. "You shouldn't trust anyone completely," Dorothy admits. "Rose, you're being naïve, don't you see, I'm stealing your money!" Rose admits, "I know Dorothy. I just hoped you'd have trouble stealing from someone who cares about you as much as I do!"

 SEASON 6

Once in St. Olaf—Originally broadcast September 29, 1990
Rose's volunteer job at the local hospital brings her face-to-face with an unexpected man from her past: Her natural born father (played by actor Don Ameche). Turns out Ameche's character got Rose's mother pregnant while he was studying to be a Franciscan monk—causing Rose to be put up for adoption. "Imagine my father, a monk who had taken a vow of silence. He made love to my mother, and didn't even call her the next day," Rose says. Rose tries for revenge—at least in her way—by tricking her father into thinking there is pie for dessert. "We have no pie, there never was any. *Now* we're even," Rose declares.

 SEASON 7

Hey, Look Me Over—Originally broadcast September 21, 1991
Rose is getting rid of some old stuff. Tops on the list is her old exercise cycle, causing her to ask Blanche, "Do you think I'm through with my cycle?" Blanche replies, "I'd say that menopause was a pretty good guess. You're about as puffy as the Pillsbury Dough Boy." Later when she's counting out some old change from a jar, she tells Sophia "I'm just going through the change." Right on cue, Sophia adds, "Well, that explains the puffiness." Sadly, Rose is appalled to learn, after developing some leftover film in an old camera, that it looks like her beloved Charlie may have slept with Blanche on a business trip to Miami many years ago. Rose tells Blanche

(with some help from Dorothy) that "you've landed on your back more than the *American Gladiators*!" and adds, "You've been under more drunken sailors that a nautical toilet!" The girls even discover, for the first time, that Blanche's initials spell out the word BED. Rose declares Blanche to be "old happy pants" but the mix-up is discovered—the film contains double-exposed images.

Where's Charlie?—Originally broadcast October 19, 1991
Miles gives Rose a friendship ring, causing her lots of doubt about whether her dearly departed husband Charlie would approve. Miles explains the ring is like a gift that Abbott may have given to Costello. "So we're like a dead comedy team?" Rose asks. As Rose shows her ring off to the girls, she says, "Look what Miles gave me!" Sophia asks, "What, liver spots?" Rose eventually decides to keep the ring—because Charlie would understand.

Dateline Miami—Originally broadcast November 2, 1991
The girls recall previous dates they'd like to forget. Rose and Blanche recall a terrible New Year's Eve—where Rose gets the lecherous guy (Lenny Wolpe) with busy hands, while Blanche ends up with the guilt-ridden virgin (Fred Willard) who wants to stay that way. Rose later recalls a terrible date with John, wonderfully portrayed by Pat Harrington, Jr. who has a plethora of former girlfriends (and at least one former boyfriend) who he has treated badly, and still show up wanting more of John's time.

Ro$e Love$ Mile$—Originally broadcast November 16, 1991
Rose has grown tired of her boyfriend Miles' cheapskate ways. Rose reports what's wrong, "It's Miles, lately he's gotten really tight." Blanche exclaims, "Oh really, I'm just the opposite. I *love* a tight man." Blanche's advice: "Dump him!" Rose declares "This is serious. Last Friday I asked him to take me someplace special. He snuck us into an AA meeting. 'Theatre of the Living' he called it, with free refreshments

afterward." Miles has even resorted to taking Rose to a bar mitzvah for free champagne. Miles is worried, it turns out, about having enough money for retirement. Rose and Miles work out a compromise—Rose can pay for meals once in awhile.

Rose: Portrait of a Woman—Originally broadcast March 7, 1992
It's Miles' birthday and Blanche convinces Rose to pose for a revealing photograph as a gift (instead of the golf clubs she originally planned for him). Rose tells Blanche she's not sure: "I'd feel cheap. I'd feel . . . well, like you!" Blanche tries to reassure her—she even uses the pictures on her Christmas cards. Dorothy recalls Blanche's card well: "The three wise men and Blanche in a teddy following the north star!" Trouble surfaces when Miles opens the gift in front of all of his university colleagues, embarrassing Rose. Miles tells Rose, "When you're young and beautiful, it's an accident of nature. When you're beautiful and older, you've earned it—that is something you created yourself!"

Home Again, Rose—Originally broadcast April 25 and May 2, 1992
A special two-part episode in which the girls cook up a scheme to crash a class reunion since Rose missed hers back in St. Olaf. The girls swipe unclaimed name tags off the sign-in table, including Rose who ends up with Kim Fong Toy, the school's Korean exchange student. When a classmate notes Rose looks different than he recalls, Rose utters one of her great lines in an Asian accent: "Different on outside, same on inside." Eventually, the plan falls apart and the girls are confronted—and Rose faints. "You see what you've done! You've upset Kim Fong Toy," Dorothy declares, not understanding Rose has truly collapsed from a heart attack. The girls wait out Rose's mishap and eventually welcome her home, but not before promising to have their head's frozen when they die. Rose says she's serious: "I want to preserve my brain!" (causing a hearty laugh among Blanche, Dorothy and Sophia).

6

A ROSE BY ANY OTHER NAME

ROSE-WORTHY MOMENTS

Perhaps most noted for her St. Olaf stories, the character Rose Nylund wasn't a one-trick pony. She was often the center of, or butt of, many a joke or putdown. But as Betty noted, Rose didn't seem to understand the blunt nature of what Dorothy, Blanche or Sophia said to her, so her feelings remained mostly intact.

"Rose had a heart of gold, but a Viking temper," Betty believes. "She had her own private agenda to life." [179]

Regardless, there was no getting around some incredibly funny moments inspired by Rose's "agenda"—

ON THE PHONE

Rose:	"I've just been talking on the phone for half an hour, and guess what?"
Blanche:	"You forgot to dial first?"
Rose:	"No!"

Dorothy:	"You held the receiver upside down?"
Rose:	"Uh-huh."
Dorothy:	"It wasn't even the phone, it was the TV remote control?"
Rose:	"No!"
Blanche:	"A shoe?"
Rose:	"Blanche, please. I'm not an idiot . . . the TV has a remote control?"

ON HER PARENTS' SEX LIFE

Rose:	"I would have died if I had ever walked in on my parents having sex."
Dorothy:	"What, you never walked in on them?"
Rose:	"Once, but they were only playing leap frog."

ON PMS

Rose:	"I never had PMS. But I did have a BMW one time."

ON BIRTHING CENTERS
[A loud scream is heard]

Birthing Center Woman:	"It sounds like there's a mommy in the making!"
Rose:	"It sounds like there's a mommy on *fire*!"
Dorothy:	"What kind of idiot would want to give birth here?"
Rose:	"This place makes me want to run out and get pregnant!"

ON THE LIMITATIONS OF NATURE

Rose:	"That's why the brown bear and the field mouse can share their love and live together in harmony. Of course, they can't mate or the mouse would explode."

ON FIRST IMPRESSIONS

Blanche: "What was your first impression of me?"

Rose: "I thought you wore too much makeup and were a slut. I was wrong. You don't wear too much makeup."

ON IRONING
(Sophia flashes Rose)

Rose: "Is it just me, or does Sophia's dress really need an ironing?"

ON ASKING QUESTIONS

Rose: "Can I ask a dumb question?"

Dorothy: "Better than anyone I know."

ON FLIRTING

Blanche: "Look at how shameless she flirts with him!"

Rose: "But Blanche, you were flirting with him too."

Blanche: "I know, but flirting is part of my heritage."

Rose: "What does that mean?"

Dorothy: "It means her mother was also a slut."

ON THE MALE PHYSIQUE

Dorothy: "Stan and I went through a totally passionless period. I totally cut off his sex."

Rose: "You mean it grows back?"

ON FEMININE HYGIENE

Blanche: "You know, a lot of those European girls don't shave under their arms."

Rose: "Is that true?"

Blanche: "They just let it all hang out."

Rose: "Really?"

Blanche: "Bushy as can be."

Rose: "Well, what do they look like in a strapless dress?"

Dorothy: "Like Milton Berle."

ON NOT GETTING A MAN TO BED

Rose: "I have a story to end all stories about when someone wouldn't sleep with me."

Blanche: "OK Honey, but *please* keep it in 10 words or less."

Rose: "OK. I will."

Dorothy: "OK then Rose, let's hear it. In 10 words or less, when did a man not sleep with you?"

Rose: "The time I was radioactive."

ON FEELINGS AROUSED DURING A WEDDING

Rose: "Am I the only one here who feels like taking off all her clothes and doing the hokey pokey?"

ON HER OWN FIGURE

Rose: "Just because I'm built like this, you wouldn't believe how many people think I'm dumb."

Sophia: "Rose, you're too hard on yourself. I know people who think you're dumb over the phone."

ON BEING FROM FARM COUNTRY

Rose: "I'm from St. Olaf. St. Olaf is farm country. We're rough and rugged. In fact, we never see doctors. Never. In fact, my great grandfather once removed his neighbor's appendix and he wasn't even sick!"

Dorothy: "Why did he do that?"

Rose: "Let's just say that they were playing poker, and the stakes got a little high."

ON GREAT LITERATURE–OR BLANCHE'S DIARY

Rose: "Once I read your diary."
Blanche: "You did what?!"
Rose: "Well, it was an accident. You left it open on the kitchen table. I was 20 pages into it before I realized it wasn't a Sidney Sheldon novel."

ON RESEMBLING SOMEONE ELSE

Dorothy: "Rose, do I look like I just fell off the turnip truck!"
Rose: "No, but you do look the woman who used to drive it."

ON BEING BACK IN ST. OLAF

Rose: "This reminds me of something that happened back in St. Olaf."
Dorothy: "Oh, Rose, stop! Rose, why is it that every time one of us makes an observation, the first thing we hear from you is 'Back in St. Olaf?' I mean, did it ever occur to you that maybe we're tired of hearing 'Back in St. Olaf,' 'Back in St. Olaf,' 'Back in St. Olaf!'
Rose: "Gee, no, I . . . I'm sorry."
Dorothy: "Oh . . . that's OK."
Rose: "Back in that town whose name you're tired of hearing . . . "
Dorothy: "ROSE!"

ON BEING HOMESICK

Rose: "Back where I come from, most people won't eat store-bought cake."
Dorothy: "Rose, back where you come from, people live in windmills and make love to polka music."
Rose: "Stop it, Dorothy. You're making me homesick!"

ON A ST. OLAF LANDMARK

Dorothy: "After a while, you feel like you're in this gigantic, black hole."

Rose: "We had a gigantic black hole back in St. Olaf."

Sophia: "Oh, God!"

Rose: "Right in front of the courthouse where Charlie and I got our marriage license, and our permit to have kids. Oh, it was a lovely hole. Everybody in town would stand around and look into it."

Dorothy: "And they say Hollywood is the entertainment capital of the world!"

Rose: "Well, sometimes they didn't just look. Sometimes, we'd point too. Or spit and then time it. And then there was the guy who'd always unzip himself . . . "

ON TRYING TO RELAX

Dorothy: "Rose, what are you listening to?"

Rose: "A relaxation tape. The sound of rain is supposed to relax me."

Dorothy: "Is it working?"

Rose: "Not really. I keep worrying that I left my car windows down."

ON LAW AND ORDER

Rose: "The laws in St. Olaf are very stringent. Their motto is 'Use a gun, go apologize.'"

ON ANSWERING A RIDDLE

Dorothy: "Blanche! How can you tell a slut from a yearbook?"

Rose: "Oh, I know! You don't have to buy a yearbook dinner."

Blanche: "Rose . . . "

Rose: "You can take a yearbook home to meet your parents."

Blanche: "Rose . . ."
Rose: "There's nothing wrong with having a yearbook on the coffee table!"
Dorothy: "Rose! This isn't a riddle!"
Rose: "Well make it one! I had three good answers!"

ON MODERN FASHION

Blanche: "I don't look right in American clothes. I have a more European physique."
Rose: "Oh? In Europe do they have big butts, too?"

ON BEING GAY

Dorothy: "Rose, I wasn't even sure you would know what a lesbian was!"
Rose: "Well, I could have looked it up!"

ON AGING

Rose: "My mother always used to say, the older you get, the better you get. Unless you're a banana."

ON BIRTHDAYS

Rose: "Oh, Blanche, if your 21st birthday was 20 years ago, you'd only be 41 years old!"
Blanche: "That's right."
Rose: "Gee, you look terrible for your age."

ON DEATH AND DYING

Sophia: "Esther Weinstock is dead. We grew up together, she was my best friend."
Dorothy: "I'm so sorry. What happened?"
Sophia: "She was fighting an oil rig fire in the Gulf of Mexico . . . SHE WAS 88!"

Rose: "Well, it's great that she was able to work right up to the end."

ON GETTING OVER DEPRESSION

Rose: "Boy, I remember when I was a little girl and we'd get depressed. Grandma could always cheer us up. She'd take out her dentures, take a healthy swig from the aquarium, then she'd put a flashlight under her chin and we would watch the gold fish swim from cheek to cheek! We could have watched it all day, but visiting hours were only from 10 to 4."

ON PLAYING THE TUBA

Rose: "I remember my mother making me practice playing the tuba. Three hours a day, seven days a week for 10 years! Oh, I hated it. But, it finally paid off."

Blanche: "I didn't know you played the tuba."

Rose: "Oh, I don't. No, I gave it up. But I can blow 32 pounds of air into a tire in less than a minute!"

ON HIGHER EDUCATION

Miles Webber: "I'm a college professor, Rose. What did you think when I said I taught Hemingway?"

Rose: "I thought you were old."

ON TALKING TO CLOWNS

Rose: "Excuse me, Mr. Clown, but could you do something funny to put a smile on the faces of three gloomy gusses?"

Clown: "Buzz off, lady. I'm on a cigarette break!"

ON OFFERING TO HELP

Rose: "Well, I'm here if you want to pick my brain."

Dorothy: "Rose, honey. Maybe we should leave it alone and let it heal."

ON TELLING A LIE

Blanche: "Just tell him you have a lot of work at home."

Rose: "I don't want to lie."

Blanche: "When you get home, we'll make you clean out the garage."

Rose: "Oh, thank you Blanche!"

ON CUTTING SCHOOL

Rose: "I don't think lying is really a good idea. I once cut school and that proved very bad."

Dorothy: "Oh, Rose. We've all cut school. It couldn't have been that bad."

Rose: "Oh, yes it was! Turns out, that was the day they taught EVERYTHING!"

Dorothy: "The final piece of the puzzle."

ON SCHOOL DAYS GONE BY

Rose: "We weren't allowed to wear berets at my school, it was against the St. Olaf dress code. They did let me wear a paper cap, though. It was long and pointy."

ON PROBLEMS WITH FARM ANIMALS

Rose: "Oh, I've known some major disappointment in this life."

Dorothy: "Rose, you're not going to tell us about that exploding pig again, are you?"

Rose: "I never told you a story about an exploding pig, Dorothy. It was a peg-legged pig. Our opossum was the one that exploded."

Dorothy: "I'm sorry Rose. There's been so many opossum explosions lately that it's hard to keep track."

ON LIFE'S DISAPPOINTMENTS

Blanche: "So what was this big disappointment in your life?"

Rose: "Butter. I wanted to be Butter Queen. It was our town's highest honor. From the time I was born, my parents groomed me for it. Singing lessons, dancing lessons, junior butter queen contests. The first 16 years of my life were all about butter!"

Dorothy: "You were very lucky. So many of us wasted our youth."

Rose: "When the time came for the pageant. I was incredible. I showed poise in the evening gown competition. I was brilliant in the oral butter quiz. They couldn't even trip me up with a trick margarine question. That evening butter was spelled R-O-S-E!"

Dorothy: "Rose, you're embarrassing yourself, please don't go on."

Rose: "I have to Dorothy, I've kept these bitter butter memories in for too long!"

ON GETTING A GOOD JOB

Rose: "I found one wonderful job, assistant manager in a pet shop. But they wouldn't hire me. I don't know why. I worked in a pet shop in St. Olaf for 10 years. I was the one who thought up big squeaky toys for cows."

ON LITTLE YIMMINY

Dorothy: "Oh . . . but you thought we *would* be interested in the story of little Yimminy, the boy who was raised by a moose . . . "

Rose: "I would point out, that moose not only raised little Yimminy, he put him through medical school!"

ON POTATO CHIPS

Rose: "I never eat chips. I don't like 'em. They fall in my bra."

ON HER HERITAGE

Blanche: "The Great Herring War?"

Rose: "Between the Lindstrom's and the Johannsen's."

Dorothy: "Oh, *that* Great Herring War!"

ON COUSIN INGMAR

Rose: "Now, I know no one wants to hear any of my stories right now . . . "

Dorothy: "That's always a safe bet, Rose."

Rose: " . . . but you need to hear about my cousin Ingmar. He was different. He used to do bird imitations."

Blanche: "Well, what's wrong with that?"

Rose: "Well, let's just say you wouldn't want to park your car under their oak tree."

ON TRYING TO GET YOUR MINKS TO BREED

Dorothy: "What they need is an aphrodisiac."

Rose: "An African what?"

Dorothy: "An aphrodisiac, Rose. Something that makes you feel sexy . . . like Spanish Fly."

Rose: "Spanish flies?"

Dorothy: "Fly, Rose. One Fly. Spanish Fly."

Rose: "Oh, come on Dorothy. I've been to Spain. It's not the cleanest country in the world, they must have thousands of flies."

Dorothy: "It is not a fly Rose! It's a beetle!"

Rose: "They call it a fly but it's really a beetle?"

Dorothy: "Yes, Rose."

Rose: "How do they know it's Spanish?"

Dorothy: "Because it wears a little sombrero, Rose!"

ON CARE AND UPKEEP OF YOUR HERRING

Rose: "You know what they say: you can lead a herring to water, but you have to walk really fast or he'll die."

ON HELPING OTHERS OVERCOME GRIEF

Rose: "How long were Jean and Pat married?"

Dorothy: "They were together for about eight years."

Rose: "Poor thing. I wish there was something I could do . . . I know! I'll make my world-famous ice cream clown sundaes! You know, the kind with the little raisin eyes and the sugar cone caps."

Dorothy: "If that doesn't fill the void, nothing will."

ON PUBLIC TRANSPORTATION

Rose: "I can't believe my mother is out riding around on a smelly old bus. Being pushed around, harassed, possibly even mugged by hostile teenagers with bad haircuts!"

ON DENYING BEING IN DENIAL

Dorothy: "Rose, I am not in denial."

Rose: "Yes, you are. You're just denying you're in denial."

Dorothy: "Rose, honey, I am not denying I'm in denial."

Rose: "If you're not denying you're in denial, then you're in denial."

Dorothy: "Look, fluffhead. Why should I deny being in denial? I never said I was in denial, *you* are the one who said I was in denial, and don't you deny it!"

ON BEING THOUGHTFUL

Rose: "I just had a thought . . . "

Sophia, Dorothy, Blanche: "Congratulations!"

ON THINKING

Rose: "You know, I've been thinking . . . "

Blanche: "Oh, that would explain the beads of sweat."

ON BEING LIKED

Rose: "Everybody likes me!"

Sophia: "I don't!"

Rose: "Oh, you just say that Sophia."

Sophia: *"REPEATEDLY!"*

ON BEING LIKED EVEN MORE

Rose: "You don't understand. Everyone likes me. I'm the nice one! Dorothy is the smart one, Blanche is the sexy one, Sophia is the old one, and I'm the nice one! *Everybody* likes me!"

Sophia: "The old one isn't so crazy about you."

ON CHRISTMAS

Rose: "Like we say in St. Olaf, Christmas without fruitcake is like St. Sigmund's Day without the headless boy."

A RARE ROSE RETORT

Blanche: "You know what I hate about cleaning up after parties?"

Rose: "What? Trying to find your underwear in the big pile?"

ANOTHER RARE ROSE MOMENT–WHILE CARRYING A BUCKET

Dorothy: "Aw, Rose, did you have a leak in (the ceiling of) your room too?"

Rose: "No, Dorothy. I was just milking the cow I keep in my closet. Wow, with only three hours of sleep, I can be as bitchy as you!"

Saying Goodbye to the Girls

During the seventh season of *Golden Girls*, Bea Arthur and NBC confirmed what had been rumored on and off for the better part of two years—Arthur was leaving the show at the end of the current season. For everyone who had fallen in love with the show, it was hard, if not impossible, to imagine *The Golden Girls* without Arthur's character, Dorothy.

Betty explained that "the last couple of years, Bea decided she didn't want to do situation comedy anymore. She wasn't comfortable, she wasn't happy, and some of the bloom rubbed off a little bit. I think there was a lot of life left in the show, but if someone is not happy, well, what do you do?"[180]

Arthur said it was time to go.

"I thought we've done seven great years, and I didn't think we could do any better," Arthur said years later. In an interview for Lifetime's *Intimate Portrait* series, Arthur admitted she did not enjoy working in television that much anymore, and was ready to move on.[181]

Arthur said she was frequently asked, after the show ended, whether any reunion episodes would be attempted. "But the way I see it, why would we? We're not going to get any better than we were, or top some of the great shows we did," she said.[182]

"*The Golden Girls* started to strain a bit by the end, and it wasn't as hysterical as it had been, so I thought it was time to leave," Arthur added.[183]

As the last season started production, the feelings were familiar for Betty. She had been through the final season of *The Mary Tyler Moore Show* as well.

"We knew it was the first day of the last season, and you know it puts things in an atmosphere, an air that you are aware of at all times," Betty said. "It got harder and harder as the season got shorter, it got more sentimental. We had been a family for seven years."[184]

Estelle Getty, who brought the Sophia Petrillo character into the face of everyone, said "We really became a family, and that is particularly true in show business. When you are together with people five days a week for hours on end, it's just like that."[185]

Betty's friend and NBC big-whig Grant Tinker said even with the success of *The Golden Girls*, Betty was reluctant to take too much credit. While Bea Arthur and Rue McClanahan openly stated how proud they were of the show, and how good they thought it was, Betty was more demur. She was proud—but more often than not, called herself privileged to have been a part of the show.

"The one thing that has always bothered me about Betty is that she won't ever admit that she's succeeded at anything," Tinker said. "She was always apologetic when she would get a laugh. She is just too modest and self-effacing for her own good, but she'll never change. We've teased her about that for years, but she just bats her eyes and changes the subject."[186]

While she may be shy or unwilling to admit how very, very good *The Golden Girls* series was, Betty is able to admit its impact on her life: "You can't walk through an airport, when you check your luggage, the skycap hugs you, which is lovely."[187]

Betty was particularly moved by young children and teenagers who liked the show. "Some of the kids grew up with me because their parents also grew up with me, and in many cases their grandparents," she said. "I've been around as a fixture. When I do a book signing, the kids come up and they weren't even born when *Mary Tyler Moore* came on or even when *Golden Girls* was on the air."[188]

Again, though, Betty credits it all to "good writing. The writing on both of those shows, that's what keeps bringing them back and makes them more for any generation, because they're funny," she said.[189]

Looking Back on the Gold

During a June 2003 Lifetime TV special, *The Golden Girls: Their Greatest Memories*, Betty joined co-stars Bea Arthur and Rue McClanahan in remembering their favorite parts of the show. By then, *Golden Girls* had quickly grown to be the most popular show on the Lifetime cable network—at one point the network airing seven episodes of the show each day.

"For seven wonderful years, I shared the screen with three unforgettable women," Betty said in opening the show. "A wise-cracking substitute school teacher, an over-sexed ego-maniac, and a feisty old lady who had a mouth like a sailor."[190]

Betty explained to viewers that this special was a chance for each of the girls—sans Estelle Getty—to highlight their favorite parts. "Estelle has retired from show business, so she won't be joining us tonight," Betty said.[191]

During the show, the girls gave details of their "Royal Command Performance" in London, England at the request of the Queen Mother—a fan of the show. "We had to learn all the protocol. We had to learn to curtsey . . . and they told us not to start any conversation, only to respond," Betty said.[192]

Betty also explained how she was recruited to get Bob Hope to guest star in an episode of *Golden Girls* where the gals were putting on a variety show for charity. It provided an opportunity to showcase some of the big stars that had visited the *Golden Girls* set besides Hope: Don Ameche, Ken Berry, Sonny Bono, George Clooney, Deana Dietrich, Howard Duff, Alice Ghostley, Polly Holliday, Mario Lopez, Kristy McNichol, Dinah Manoff, Richard Mulligan, Lesley Nielson, Jerry Orbach, Burt Reynolds, Debbie Reynolds, Cesar Romero, Mickey Rooney, Lyle Waggoner, and Nancy Walker.

The Lifetime TV special also gave viewers a rare glimpse of publicity-shy *Golden Girls* creator and writer, Susan Harris. From a 1989 interview, she noted that she wanted to do the show because "Women have a different perspective. Women laugh at different things. And being a woman, you tend to look at things that way. So yes, there definitely was a woman's voice. I believe that women are more attuned to people in a human way then men are. Women tend to look more at the person, at who really resides there, and they are better able to represent the characters."[193]

Harris and her interaction with the show—slowed by her reported struggles with chronic fatigue syndrome (a disease written into story line for Dorothy's character), "is a very strange and talented person," Betty said. "She was upset when some of the writers got an Emmy before her, so she never wanted to write for us again."[194]

Jim Colucci, TV writer and author of the book, *The Q Guide to the Golden Girls,* noted that "by the summer of 2006—14 years after *The Golden Girls* ended its original run, the show was still drawing 11 million viewers per week and 30 million per month on the Lifetime cable network, its home since 1997. Although up against much newer sitcom competition, any one of the show's seven daily airings still ranked among the top three 'off network' sitcoms shown by Lifetime, and among the top seven on any cable channel."[195]

Enter the Golden Palace

Betty was aware of swirling rumors that Bea Arthur—and perhaps even Estelle Getty—planned to leave the show as early as after the fourth season. Their departure would have devastated the show, certainly, but would not have been a result of any friction on the set. "It's a fun (cast) and a happy group," Betty said. "I think the reason we all get along so well is we're four different points on a compass. You couldn't put four women together who are more diverse than the four of us . . . We're a united front and we all stand together."[196]

As it turned out, Getty stayed on board after season seven, as Arthur's character Dorothy was married off and written out of the new CBS spin-off, *The Golden Palace*. *Golden Girls* creator Susan Harris also was the driving force behind *The Golden Palace*. The show took its name from a local Miami Beach hotel the remaining girls—Blanche, Rose and Sophia—purchased after Dorothy's marriage.

Betty believed the premise of *The Golden Palace* was a good one—taking the girls out of a "cloistered environment" that seven years inside Blanche's Miami home had created, and instead, letting the world come to them and interact with them.

"(*The Golden Palace*) would take them outside of their regular selves, and that was a good idea," Betty said. "The problem was we had the same writers as on *The Golden Girls*, and pretty soon if a script or a storyline was not working out, we (reverted) to doing *Golden Girls* in the lobby (of the hotel) which was not the idea that Susan (Harris) had. I think that's why we only lasted one year. It's like taking a leg off a four-legged table. If you take one leg away, you might be able to balance it, but the table doesn't seem very steady."[197]

For her part, McClanahan said she had her doubts about *Golden Palace* from the start. "I thought we should get a roommate to replace Dorothy, there were a lot of wonderfully talented comedy actresses out there," McClanahan wrote in her memoir.[198]

Regardless of the doubts, the group sans Bea Arthur trudged forward, although she appeared in a two-part episode titled "Seems Like Old Times" where she expresses worry that Sophia is too old to be working in a beachfront hotel.

Sometimes derisively referred to as "the eighth season" of the *Golden Girls*, Betty admits that *Golden Palace* "was too much of trying to do the same old *Golden Girls*, but without all four of us, and it was not balanced. The idea was sound to make them to have to attend to some modern problems, but I don't think the writers were prepared for it."

Further complicating matters, *Golden Palace* bounced around on the CBS primetime schedule (abandoning the *Girls'* established slot on Saturday night on NBC). Eventually it landed in a tough time slot on Friday nights against ABC's established hit *Family Matters*, *The Golden Palace* scored some early ratings success (perhaps out of curiosity from viewers) and added new characters—showcasing actors Don Cheadle and Cheech Marin—but ended after 24 episodes at the close of the 1993 television season.

The Last Golden Girl

Although the oldest of the four women who made *Golden Girls* a TV legend, Betty outlived each of the other members of the cast—Estelle Getty passed away in 2008, Bea Arthur in 2009, and Rue McClanahan in 2010.

Getty's passing came on July 22, 2008 at her home just three days before her 85th birthday. Getty succumbed after a long and difficult struggle with Lewy Body Dementia, a progressive brain disease.

A minor controversy arose among tabloid reporters when it was learned that Betty, Bea Arthur and Rue McClanahan did not plan to attend the funeral. Getty's son, Carl Gettleman, told *Inside Edition* that he was disappointed by the "no show."

For the last time together in public, three of NBC's *Golden Girls* pause on the red carpet for the June 2008 TV Land Awards. Bea Arthur, at left, leaned on co-star Rue McClanahan throughout the evening as her health was quickly fading. Arthur died April 25, 2009, and McClanahan passed away June 3, 2010. Estelle Getty was not present for the awards, and died less than a month later on July 22, 2008. *(Shutterstock.com/Joe Seer)*

"They certainly would have been welcome," he said. "I don't know why they wouldn't be attending mom's funeral. Maybe it's a painful thing. If it was someone I'd been tight with like that and worked with all those years, I'd have been there."[199]

Golden Girls' former executive producer, Tony Thomas, reportedly did attend.

For her part, Arthur said attending funerals was too emotional for her and that Estelle had "been out of it so many years, not recognizing anyone. (Her passing) is a godsend. She's at peace."[200]

McClanahan said from her New York home that she was unable to fly to California for the service because of a recent surgery. "I'd like (her family) to know that I didn't attend because I can't fly right now with knee surgery," McClanahan told *Inside Edition*. "I don't know why Betty and Bea didn't go, maybe because they, too, have said their goodbyes to her when she was alive."[201]

Betty was "adamant" that Getty would not have wanted her three co-stars there because of the tabloid coverage it would generate. "We were with Estelle when it mattered. I didn't go to her funeral and Paul, her wonderful caretaker, knew I wasn't going to her funeral," Betty said.[202]

She added, "Funerals are about (the media)—who was there and who wasn't? That's not about Estelle. We adored her. To tell you the truth, her passing is tough on us, but it's a blessing for her. She's been so ill for so long, she's in a better place now, wherever she is."[203]

Less than a year later, more sad news would surface—this time that Bea Arthur's brave fight against cancer had come to an end on April 25, 2009. She was 86. Betty was called upon to make several public statements. She and the only other remaining co-star, McClanahan, did interviews (mostly via phone) with all of the network morning news shows, and the syndicated entertainment shows.

Prior to her death, Arthur recalled the joy she felt when fans would recognize her: "I still have people constantly recognizing me, saying, 'Oh my God, it's Dorothy!' It is so sweet and so nice . . . After all these years, I am delighted. It is incredible when you realize, *The Golden Girls* is all over the globe."[204]

Arthur's death was felt across Hollywood and Broadway— she was just one of those unforgettable TV and film stars that everyone seemed to recall. With Arthur's deep voice and imposing 5 foot 9 inch stature—there was just no ignoring her. On New York's "Great White Way," theatre marquees went dark for one minute at 8 p.m. on April 28, 2009 in honor of Arthur's contribution to the stage.

"I knew it would hurt, I just didn't know it would hurt this much," Betty told *Entertainment Tonight* about Arthur's passing. "I'm so happy that she received her Lifetime Achievement Award while she was still with us, so she could appreciate that. She was such a big part of my life."[205]

On ABC's *Good Morning America*, Betty said one of her favorite memories of Bea Arthur was of a Monday table reading of that week's script. "One morning we read, and the script was very funny. We were giggling, and when we finished the reading of the script, we thanked the writers profusely. I can still see Bea sitting there. And she looked at me, and her eyes were twinkling, and she said, 'Aren't we lucky?' And, you know, it's something that I've hung on to all these years."[206]

Again, just over a year later came the unexpected news of Rue McClanahan's death on June 3, 2010. She was 76 and death was ruled as a result of a massive stroke subsequent to a heart bypass surgery she had earlier in the year.

Betty issued a statement about McClanahan's passing that sounded somewhat similar to what she said when Arthur died, especially related to how her grief hurt her heart. She said, "Rue was a close and dear friend. I treasured our relationship. It hurts more than I even thought it would, if that's possible."[207]

The earlier controversy about Getty's funeral was not repeated with the passing of Arthur and McClanahan—both women wanted no public observances.

True fans knew that for Estelle Getty and Rue McClanahan—*Golden Girls* was perhaps their greatest acting achievement. Betty and Bea Arthur had both had other successes on TV, but for Getty and McClanahan—*Golden Girls* was the top of their mountain. "I knew from the moment I opened the envelope and saw *The Golden Girls* written on the cover (of the script) in cursive typeface that it would be a hit," McClanahan said.[208]

7

Moving On From Miami

At the end of *The Golden Palace*, Betty hardly took a breath after her now eight-year run as Rose Nylund of Miami was coming to an end. In the fall 1993, she was a new cast member in Bob Newhart's third (and ultimately ill-fated) sitcom effort on CBS in a show simply titled, *Bob*. The show built around Newhart's straight-man delivery as a comic book designer, found Betty as "Sylvia Schmidt," Bob's boss. Despite everyone's best effort—with the exception, perhaps of CBS, who moved the show from Friday to Monday and back to Friday again, *Bob* left the air in December 1993—a ratings failure. It was a rare miss for Newhart—and for Betty.

Maybe This Time?

Betty didn't stay down long. In September 1995, one year after leaving *Bob* behind among canceled CBS shows, ABC bought a show from veteran producers Michael Jacobs and Bob Young (producers of another ABC hit, *Boy Meets World*).

Built as a vehicle for Marie Osmond, Betty was brought on board to play the mother of Marie's character. *Maybe This Time*, as the show was eventually named, told the story of three generations of women in one family depicted by Betty, Marie and a young child star, Ashley Johnson.

Betty said on *Larry King Live* that it was the involvement of Osmond that attracted her to the show. Betty said she went into a meeting to discuss the show and prepared to say no to another try at series TV. "Marie Osmond is a delight," Betty said.[209]

Even so, in a rare "off moment" Betty couldn't think of why the show was given the name it had—*Maybe This Time*—and so she and King agreed to move on in an awkward satellite interview. Betty did like the show's proposed timeslot—on ABC's Saturday night schedule.

"I'm back on Saturday nights," she said. "Everyone said, 'Oh, that's a tough night.' It wasn't for some of my other shows."[210]

ABC promoted the show as starring "America's sweetheart" Marie Osmond and "America's Golden Girl" Betty White.

A personal highlight for Betty was the surprise appearance of *Golden Girls* co-star Estelle Getty in the audience for the taping of the premiere episode of *Maybe This Time*. It was a rare highlight—the show got off to a hot-start, placing in the top 20 Nielson ratings for its first week, but quickly fell. Ultimately, *Maybe This Time* suffered in the ratings and was canceled by ABC in February 1996 after just 18 episodes.

On The Ladies Man

Betty returned to series TV in 1999 with the launch of a new CBS sitcom, *The Ladies Man*, starring British-born actor Alfred Molina who lives in one house surrounded by his mother, wife, ex-wife, mother-in-law, and daughter.

Betty poses next to her wax likeness at the Madame Tussaud Museum in Hollywood in June 2012. *(Shutterstock.com/Joe Seer)*

The CBS marketing department said Molina's character Jimmy Stiles was "prone to making tactless conversation" and "unintentionally insults his wife, Donna (played by Sharon Lawrence), on a regular basis." Complicating matters, Jimmy gets no help from his mom, Mitzi, played by Betty, who delights in recounting numerous embarrassing escapades from Jimmy's childhood.

The show also featured *Designing Women* alumna Dixie Carter in the role of Peaches (as Jimmy's meddling mother-in-law). Add in his 10-year-old daughter and another daughter from his first marriage, and Jimmy is greatly outnumbered.

Critics seemed to tolerate the show—and CBS executives were kind to it, normally scheduling it in their Monday night block of established comedy shows. Nevertheless, as is the case with many modern sitcoms, it was not a "break out" hit gaining a lot of notice from viewers or insiders, and after 30 episodes CBS did not renew the show after the 2000-01 season. Initially announced by CBS as cancelled in 2000, the show came back slightly reworked in new episodes broadcast during the summer of 2001. The show finally ended there in June 2001.

In the series, Betty played Mitzi Stiles, the ever-present and always talking mom to Molina's Jimmy character. *Designing*

Women alum Dixie Carter joined the show in later episodes as Jimmy's mother-in-law, Peaches.

While *Ladies Man* was a mostly forgettable effort—the show did serve to reunite Betty with *Golden Girls'* co-stars Rue McClanahan (who appeared in two episodes), and Estelle Getty (who appeared in one episode—her very last appearance on primetime television prior to her death in 2008).

Boston Legal and the Murderous Catherine Piper

Producer-director David E. Kelley brought *Boston Legal* to ABC in 2004 as a spinoff of another successful ABC dramedy, *The Practice*. *Boston Legal*, which served to help revive the sagging primetime fortunes of several stars (including James Spader, William Shatner and Candice Bergen), was a cult-classic hit just like *The Practice*.

Betty showed up in season 2 of *Boston Legal* after three previous guest spots on *The Practice*. Her character, Catherine Piper, is described as a gossipy, calculating character that viewers loved. The edginess of the Catherine character fit Betty well. Catherine's antics were nothing short of incredible—accused of killing a man by whacking him in the head with an iron skillet, as well as accusations of armed robbery and abducting an old woman from a sub-standard nursing home. None of the charges stuck, and Catherine's character came into and out of the law firm's life as both an employee (later fired, and rehired), and a client (she was an acquitted murder defendant, after all).

Boston Legal lasted 101 episodes—Betty's wild-eyed character Catherine appeared in 16 episodes of those until it was canceled by ABC in December 2008. Betty's final appearance was in an episode titled "Juiced" and showed her character blowing up her doctor's medical office (and killing the doctor in the process) as revenge for having received the wrong prescription medicine.

Appearing on *Boston Legal* was "such fun. It is a great group of people on both sides of the camera. You saw me commit murder and get away with it. You saw me rob a convenience store, and you saw me kidnap my friend out of a nursing home. I thought David E. Kelley had run out of crime for me to do, but then I set my doctor's office on fire and blew him up."[211]

Betty and the 'One Spot'

No other Hollywood actor ever made more out of a "one spot" or single guest star appearance than did Betty White. She parlayed one of her early "one spot" opportunities—as Sue Ann Nivens on *The Mary Tyler Moore Show*, into a recurring character that eventually appeared in 39 episodes. Her success on MTM must have inspired her as she accepted bit parts in tons other TV hits along the way, including this impressive list:

- *Pound Puppies*, Hub, 2012—as voice of Agatha
- *The Client List*, Lifetime, 2012—as Ruth Hudson
- *Hallmark Hall of Fame: The Lost Valentine*, CBS, 2011—as Caroline Thomas
- *Community*, NBC, 2010—as Professor June Bauer
- *You Again?* NBC, 2010—as Grandma Bunny
- *The Middle*, ABC, 2010—as Mrs. Nethercott
- *30 Rock*, NBC, 2009—as herself
- *Glenn Martin, D.D.S.*, Nickelodeon, 2009—as voice of Dora
- *Kathy Griffin: My Life on the D List*, Bravo, 2009—as herself
- *My Name is Earl*, NBC, 2009—as Mrs. Weezmer
- *Ugly Betty*, ABC, 2007—as herself
- *The Simpsons*, Fox, 2007 (and 2000)—voice of herself
- *My First Time*, NBC, 2006—as herself

- 📺 *Family Guy*, Fox, 2006—as voice of herself
- 📺 *Joey*, NBC, 2005—as Mrs. Bly
- 📺 *Complete Savages*, ABC, 2004-05—two episodes as Mrs. Riley
- 📺 *Father of the Pride*, NBC, 2004—two episodes as Grandma Wilson
- 📺 *Malcolm in the Middle*, Fox, 2004—as Sylvia
- 📺 *My Wife and Kids*, ABC, 2004—as Mrs. June Hopkins
- 📺 *Everwood*, WB, 2004—two episodes as Carol Roberts
- 📺 *Higglytown Heroes*, Disney Network, 2003-07—three episodes as the voice of Grandma
- 📺 *Gary the Rat*, Spike, 2003—two episodes as the voice of Gary's mother
- 📺 *The Crime Adventures of Billy and Mandy*, Cartoon Network, 2003—voice of Mrs. Doolin
- 📺 *Bringing Down the House*, ABC Family, 2003—as Mrs. Kline
- 📺 *That '70s Show*, Fox, 2002-03—four episodes as Bea Sirgudson
- 📺 *Providence*, NBC, 2002—as Julianna
- 📺 *Yes, Dear*, CBS, 2002—as Sylvia
- 📺 *The Wild Thornberrys*, Nickelodeon, 2000—as Grandma Sophie
- 📺 *King of the Hill*, Fox, 1999-2002—two episodes as the voice of Dorothy and Delia
- 📺 *Ally McBeal*, Fox, 1999—as Dr. Shirley Flott
- 📺 *Hercules*, USA Network, 1999—as voice of Hestia
- 📺 *L.A. Doctors*, CBS, 1998—as Mrs. Brooks
- 📺 *Suddenly Susan*, NBC, 1996—as Midge Haber
- 📺 *Newton's Apple*, PBS, 1996—as herself
- 📺 *The John Larroquette Show*, NBC, 1996—as herself

- *The Naked Truth*, ABC, 1995—two episodes as herself
- *Diagnosis: Murder*, CBS, 1994—as Dora Sloan
- *Nurses*, NBC, 1991—as Rose Nylund
- *Carol & Company*, NBC, 1991—as Trisha Durant
- *Empty Nest,* NBC, 1989-91—as Rose Nylund
- *Matlock*, NBC, 1987—as herself
- *Who's The Boss?*, ABC, 1985—two episodes as Bobby Barnes
- *St. Elsewhere*, NBC, 1985—two episodes as Capt. Gloria Neal
- *Hotel*, ABC, 1984—as Wilma Klein
- *Fame*, NBC, 1983—as Catherine
- *Madame's Place*, syndicated, 1982—as herself
- *Love, Sidney*, NBC, 1982—as Charlotte
- *The Love Boat*, ABC, 1980-85—five episodes as Betsy Boucher
- *The Jim Nabors Show*, CBS, 1978—as herself
- *Donny & Marie*, ABC, 1978—as herself
- *The Jacksons Variety Show*, CBS, 1976—as herself
- *Ellery Queen*, NBC, 1975—as Louise Demery
- *Lucas Tanner*, NBC, 1975—as Lydia Merrick
- *The Odd Couple*, ABC, 1972—as herself
- *O'Hara: U.S. Treasury*, CBS, 1971—as herself
- *Petticoat Junction*, CBS, 1969—as Adelle Colby
- *United States Steel Hour*, CBS, 1962—as an actress
- *The Millionaire*, CBS, 1956—as Virginia Lennert

Everywhere Else on Your TV

In 2002-03, Betty appeared on four episodes of Fox's popular retro show, *That '70s Show*. On the show, she played the often-disapproving mother of the character Kitty (played by Debra Jo Rupp). In one episode, she claimed to have never gone through menopause. "I have always been quite healthy, and I always told you to eat your vegetables," she tells Kitty.

Other prime-time moments of note for Betty included:

30 Rock (NBC)	*Malcolm in the Middle* (Fox)
Alf (NBC)	*Matlock* (NBC/ABC)
Ally McBeal (Fox)	*My Name Is Earl* (NBC)
Community (NBC)	*My Wife and Kids* (ABC)
Diagnosis: Murder (CBS)	*Nurses* (NBC)
Ellen (ABC)	*Petticoat Junction* (CBS)
Ellery Queen (NBC)	*Providence* (NBC)
Empty Nest (NBC)	*Suddenly Susan* (NBC)
Everwood (WB)	*The Middle* (ABC)
Fame (NBC)	*The Odd Couple* (ABC)
Hotel (ABC)	*The U.S. Steel Hour* (CBS)
Joey (NBC)	*Ugly Betty* (ABC)
Love, Sidney (NBC)	*Who's the Boss?* (ABC)
Lucas Tanner (NBC)	*Yes, Dear* (CBS)

In this same period she picked up two "voice" roles on Fox's animated series, *King of the Hill*, and three episodes each of *The Wild Thornberrys* on Nickelodeon and *Higglytown Heroes* on The Disney Channel. Her voice also graced episodes of the more adult animated series, *The Simpsons* and *Family Guy* (both on Fox). These were just the latest of many animated series where Betty leant her talents—and her voice.

Betty did not limit herself to primetime. A long-time fan of daytime dramas—soap operas to most viewers—Betty seemingly thumbed her nose at "Hollywood rules" and readily appeared on daytime TV. Most established primetime stars shunned daytime TV as either the training ground for primetime hopefuls, or the last stop for washed up used-to-be's. Betty viewed it as another place to have fun and engage interesting characters.

In total, Betty appeared on 22 episodes of CBS' *The Bold and the Beautiful* in 2006-09 as the character Ann Douglas, and at the height of her *Golden Girls* fame, she showed up on NBC's *Santa Barbara* for three episodes and one episode of *Another World*, both in 1988.

A Very Special Betty

A lot of Hollywood stars are offered "specials" on network TV—sometimes the network wants them to help grab ratings, and sometimes the stars want a little help reviving or keeping a career going. Regardless the reason, it seems everyone wanted Betty as a "guest star" on their specials. The list of TV specials she has appeared on through the years is dizzying:

- 📺 *26th Annual Academy Awards*—1954
- 📺 *78th Annual Tournament of Roses Parade*—1967
- 📺 *The Paul Lynde Halloween Special*—1976
- 📺 *28th Annual Primetime Emmy Awards*—1976
- 📺 *Circus of the Stars*—1977
- 📺 *The Jackson's Summer Special*—1977
- 📺 *The John Davidson Christmas Special*—1977
- 📺 *Circus of the Stars*—1979
- 📺 Bob Hope's *Stand Up and Cheer for the NFL's 50th Year*—1981
- 📺 *Those Wonderful Game Shows*—1984

- *John Rivers and Friends Salute Heidi Abromowitz*—1985
- *Walt Disney World's 15th Birthday Celebration*—1986
- *America Talks Back*—1986
- *NBC's 60th Anniversary Celebration*—1986
- *The Television Academy Hall of Fame*—1986
- *Barbara Walters' Special: What is This Thing Called Love?*—1986
- *38th Annual Primetime Emmy Awards*—1986
- *13th Annual People Choice Awards*—1987
- *First Annual American Comedy Awards*—1987
- *39th Annual Primetime Emmy Awards*—1987
- *Betty White: This is Your Life!*—1987
- *Happy Birthday, Hollywood!*—1987
- *ALF Loves a Mystery*—1988
- *Happy Birthday Bob* (Hope): *50 Stars Salute 50 Years on NBC*—1988
- *The Hollywood Christmas Parade*—1988
- *The Magical World of Disney*—1988
- *Super Bloopers & Practical Jokes*—1988
- *Second Annual American Comedy Awards*—1988
- *40th Annual Primetime Emmy Awards*—1988
- *Third Annual American Comedy Awards*—1989
- *Bob Hope's Love Affair with Lucy*—1989
- *Friday Night Surprise!*—1989
- *Hanna-Barbara's 50th: A Yabba-Dabba-Doo Celebration*—1989
- *The Valvoline National Driving Test*—1989
- *The American Red Cross Emergency Test*—1990
- *NBC's Night of 100 Stars*—1990
- *Time Warner's Earth Day Special*—1990

- 📺 *The Tube Test*—1990
- 📺 *42nd Annual Primetime Emmy Awards*—1990
- 📺 *Fourth Annual American Comedy Awards*—1990
- 📺 *48th Annual Golden Globes Awards*—1991
- 📺 *Fifth Annual American Comedy Awards*—1991
- 📺 *43rd Annual Primetime Emmy Awards*—1991
- 📺 *17th Annual People's Choice Awards*—1991
- 📺 *Doris Day: A Sentimental Journey*—1991
- 📺 *Funny Women of Television: A Museum of Television & Radio Tribute*—1991
- 📺 *Mary Tyler Moore Show's 20th Anniversary Special*—1991
- 📺 *Walt Disney's Happy Easter Parade*—1991
- 📺 *Bob Hope & Other Young Comedians: The World Laughs*—1992
- 📺 *Hats Off: America Honors Minnie Pearl*—1992
- 📺 *Walt Disney's Very Merry Christmas Parade*—1992
- 📺 *Bob Hope: The First 90 Years*—1993
- 📺 *Ninth Annual Television Academy Hall of Fame*—1993
- 📺 *Bob Hope's Birthday Memories*—1994
- 📺 *Great Love Songs of All Time*—1995
- 📺 *The Story of Santa Claus*—1996
- 📺 *1996 MTV Movie Awards*—1996
- 📺 *11th Annual Television Academy Hall of Fame*—1996
- 📺 *50 Years of Television: A Celebration of the Academy of Television Arts and Sciences*—1997
- 📺 *Intimate Portrait: Mary Tyler Moore*—1997
- 📺 *Noddy Holiday Special: Anything Can Happen at Christmas*—1997
- 📺 *Behind the Laughs: The Untold Stories of Television's Favorite Comedies*—1998

- ▢ *13th Annual Television Academy Hall of Fame*—1999
- ▢ *The '70s: The Decade That Changed Television*—2000
- ▢ *26th Annual People's Choice Awards*—2000
- ▢ *14th Annual American Comedy Awards*—2000
- ▢ *Intimate Portrait: Rue McClanahan*—2000
- ▢ *Intimate Portrait: Betty White*—2000
- ▢ *Intimate Portrait: Estelle Getty*—2001
- ▢ *Disney's American Teacher Awards*—2001
- ▢ *NBC 75th Anniversary Special*—2002
- ▢ *The Mary Tyler Moore Show Reunion*—2002
- ▢ *Great Women of Television Comedy*—2003
- ▢ *Intimate Portrait: Bea Arthur*—2003
- ▢ *Real Comedy: Bringing Down the House*—2003
- ▢ *First Annual TV Land Awards*—2003
- ▢ *The Golden Girls: Their Greatest Moments*—2003
- ▢ *Lifetime Achievement Awards: Women Changing the World*—2003
- ▢ *CBS at 75*—2003
- ▢ *Intimate Portrait: Vicki Lawrence*—2003
- ▢ *Second Annual TV Land Awards*—2004
- ▢ *TV Land Moguls*—2004
- ▢ *TV's Greatest Sidekicks*—2004
- ▢ *TV's 20 Greatest Game Shows*—2005
- ▢ *The Greatest, Sexiest Southern Men*—2006
- ▢ *Comedy Central's Roast of William Shatner*—2006
- ▢ *The Real Match Game: The Story Behind the Blanks*—2006
- ▢ *Fifth Annual TV Land Awards*—2007
- ▢ *2007 Screen Actors Guild Awards*—2007
- ▢ *Pioneers of Television*—2008

- 📺 *TV Land Awards*—2008
- 📺 *American Masters: Carol Burnett*—2009
- 📺 *TV Land Awards*—2010
- 📺 *62nd Annual Emmy Awards*—2010
- 📺 *American Film Institute 39th Annual Lifetime Achievement Award Honoring Morgan Freeman*—2011
- 📺 *63rd Annual Emmy Awards*—2011
- 📺 *Betty White's 90th Birthday: A Salute to America's Golden Girl*—2012
- 📺 *64th Annual Emmy Awards*—2012

Two of her "special" appearances went so well, she came back every year—including a two-decade run from 1970-90 as the co-host of NBC telecast of the Tournament of Roses Parade each January from Pasadena, California. She also was tapped to co-host with Bob Hope and others NBC's coverage of the Macy's Thanksgiving Day Parade for a decade from 1980-90.

BETTY THE AUTHOR

In 1987, Betty finally sat down and released her very first book, *Betty White in Person*. On an appearance on both NBC's *Tonight Show Starring Johnny Carson* and The Nashville Network's *Dinah!*—Dinah Shore's latest daytime TV show—the stars admitted "leafing through" the book. It wasn't a heavy read, mostly stories and observations from a Hollywood veteran, or as she put it, "my frame of reference."

Carson told Betty that he had expected more of a Shelley Winters' style "Hollywood tell all" book.

"It's not that kind of book," Betty said. "It's a series of little vignettes."[212]

A recurring member of the "Mighty Carson Art Players," Betty portrays Jane to Johnny Carson's Tarzan in this 1981 sketch on NBC's *The Tonight Show*. The gag was Betty and Johnny were a not-so-happily married jungle-duo observing their 25th anniversary as "Me Tarzan, you Jane." *(AP Photo)*

Carson admitted the book helped him learn more about Betty. "I feel like I've known you for many years, but I'm not sure I know you that well."

Always quick on her feet, Betty replied: "Well, maybe if you hadn't been in such a rush to get married, we could have worked something out."[213]

Her book hawking appearance on *The Tonight Show* was nothing new. Betty had appeared many times with Jack Paar during the show's earlier run, and had recurring appearances with Carson as part of his "Mighty Carson Art Players." In fact, Betty and Carson created some of the show's most memorable skits—both variations on the same theme: Adam and Eve 25 years into their marriage, and later, Tarzan and Jane 20-plus years into marriage. Betty said the Tarzan and Jane bits represented "a couple who had been in the jungle just a little too long."

In the years since, Betty has penned six other books, reflecting her love of the written word. Interestingly, the last two books she released in 2012, *If You Ask Me (And of Course You Won't)* and *Betty & Friends: My Life at the Zoo* have been among her best-sellers. Other titles have included *Here We Go: My Life in Television* (1997 and re-released in 2010), *Betty White in Person* (re-released in 2011), and two-co-authorships with Tom Sullivan, *Together: A Story of Shared Vision* (2009) and *The Leading Lady: Dinah's Story* (1991).

What the Tabloids Say

Bad news about Betty has been rare—and perhaps not surprisingly, it has come mostly in the form of tabloid "news" reports. Just as Betty's late-life career was enjoying a huge rise, reports surfaced that Betty was allegedly estranged from one of her stepchildren, Martha Ludden, daughter of Allen Ludden.

A close-up look at Betty and her wax double at Madame Tussaud's in Hollywood. *(Shutterstock.com/Joe Seer)*

Tabloid reports indicated Martha was unhappy about the attention Betty took from her father away from the children, and that she engaged in teenage rebellion to get her father's attention. "A source told the *National Enquirer* that Allen used to argue with Martha constantly over her . . . anger towards Betty. Her tumultuous relationship with her father caused him a lot of grief."[214]

The Enquirer's "insider source" said "I think Betty blamed Martha for making Allen's last years nothing but misery and heartache."[215]

Martha herself told *The Enquirer* that, "The last time I spoke with my stepmother, Betty White, was 30 years ago."[216]

On a February 1990 appearance on the short-lived *Pat Sajak Show* on CBS, Betty engaged the topic of tabloids by calling them "bird cage newspapers" and "garbage."

"I don't feel strongly about (the tabloids), and no one ever admits to ever reading them. They always just say they looked at them in the line at the grocery store," Betty said. "What makes me the maddest are people who can't read a newspaper, or read a news magazine, or God-forbid, a book, but they read (the tabloids) and then quote it chapter and verse, as if that was it."[217]

She noted how wrong the tabloids always seemed to get it: "Every second week they have one of the *Golden Girls* stomping off the set because one makes more money than the other, or someone is sleeping with someone else's things."[218]

New York Magazine writer Willa Paskin posed an interesting idea, that "in the court of public opinion, it is currently illegal to make fun of Betty White. She is a lovable national treasure, possessed with a wonderful attitude, work ethic, and sense of comic timing." As a result, Paskin said, critics were overly kind to her performances on *Hot in Cleveland*. White had become "a protected category of person: too awesome, too funny, too old, and too condescended to be respectfully (or not so respectfully) criticized," Paskin said.[219]

There are other critics as well—including, perhaps surprisingly, veterinarians. *DVM Newsmagazine* surveyed its readers in 2012, and lingering resentment appears to remain for Betty's 2007 TV ad for 1-800-PetMeds, an online veterinary medicine retailer. In the 2007 ad, the company's tag line "I saved a trip to the vet!" was delivered by Betty. The magazine reported that "some veterinarians, concerned about what they perceive as their declining reputation among pet owners, point to White and PetMeds Express as the cause."[220]

A spokesman for 1-800-PetMeds, Rich Herch, notes that "Betty did a commercial for PetMeds years ago, which we terminated as soon as we found out how vets felt about PetMeds."

Herch added, "Betty loves veterinarians and would never knowingly do anything that would be perceived as something contrary."[221]

Steve Dale, an animal rights writer and journalist, defends Betty and her involvement with the PetMeds ad. He suggests that it remains so much in the minds of viewers, even years after it left the air, because of her high credibility among viewers for her love of animals. "I don't believe that there is a celebrity on the planet who has done more to promote the plight of companion animals and wildlife than Betty White," Dale said.[222]

8

Fun And Games With Betty

The Competitive Nature of Betty

Betty White once confessed to reporters that her own personality was a little closer to that of her character Rose Nylund on *The Golden Girls* than perhaps most people knew. Like Rose, Betty is a fierce competitor.

For Betty, it's not "just a game"—"You're doing your best, and it's mental exercise."[223]

"I've done every television game show that's been done," Betty declares. She noted that she and her parents would sit around the breakfast table playing games. "I get uptight with people who say, 'Who cares? It's only a game.'"[224]

Some have joked that it may be easier to make a list of game shows Betty *hasn't* appeared on—the list of game shows she has graced is perhaps unmatched in Hollywood lore.

Mark Goodson, one half of the game-show powerhouse partnership of Goodson-Todman, said "as a player Betty was very good, almost always had the right answers. And when she wasn't right, she was never at a loss for words, and in our business, words are worth a lot."[225]

"We first met Betty when we were children on *Make the Connection* in the 1950s," Goodson said. "Betty was so wonderful and we booked her for everything after that. The most important show we ever booked her on was in 1961, a show we called *Password* hosted by Allen Ludden."[226]

NBC's *Make the Connection* dates back to the earliest days of television and represented Betty's first game show appearance as a panelist. Originally hosted by Jim McKay (who went on to become the familiar face of ABC Sports in subsequent Olympic broadcasts), hosting duties eventually fell to Gene Rayburn, someone destined to become one of Betty's best Hollywood friends. Formatted a lot like the successful *I've Got a Secret* over on CBS, *Make the Connection* and *I've Got a Secret* both emanated from the television production studios of Goodson-Todman.

Game shows were a natural fit for Betty. Regular appearances soon racked up on a variety of other game shows, including *Password Plus*, *Super Password*, *What's My Line?*, *To Tell the Truth*, *Liar's Club*, *Celebrity Double Talk*, *Animal Crack-Ups*, *Sweethearts*, *$25,000 Pyramid*, *$100,000 Pyramid*, and even *I've Got A Secret.* In the summer of 2006, she joined a parade of CBS stars for *Game Show Marathon* and appeared in the show's *Match Game* segments. She even joined a short-lived primetime effort on CBS to revive the familiar *Password* format, this time with *Million Dollar Password* in 2008-09, hosted by Regis Philbin. Sadly, no contestant ever won the top prize—$1 million in this, the latest resurrection of *Password*.

The full list of game shows Betty appeared on over the years is amazing:

$10,000 Pyramid

$100,000 Pyramid

$25,000 Pyramid

Animal Crack-Ups

Best of Family Feud

Celebrity Double Talk

Celebrity Family Feud

Celebrity Sweepstakes

Dick Haynes' Joke Shop

Family Feud

Girl Talk

Grab Your Phone!

H2: Hollywood Squares

Hollywood Squares

I've Got a Secret

Just Men!

Liar's Club

Make the Connection

Match Game

Match Game P.M.

Million Dollar Password

Password

Password Plus

Snap Judgment

Super Password

Tattle Tales

The New Hollywood Squares

The New Liar's Club

To Tell the Truth

What's My Line?

Win, Lose or Draw

You Don't Say

Make the Connection

Betty soon became a regular on *Make the Connection*, dubbed TV's "most lively panel show"—presented by Borden's Dairy. The show only aired, however, about three months on NBC's Thursday night line-up in 1955, but it gained respectable notices for both Betty and its moderator—"the bright young TV comedian" Gene Rayburn.

The show was only a slight variation of other shows airing on other networks. Four celebrity panelists, including Betty, had to guess the connection between an everyday person and another celebrity. In one episode, silent film star and comic great Buster

Betty's love of games was for real—not just for the cameras. Pictured here in April 1965 with her husband and *Password* host Allen Ludden, the latest round in a "friendly" game of gin rummy Betty and Allen had stretched out over several years. *(AP Photo/Bob Wands)*

Keaton appeared. The audience was in on the secret—they would get to see what the connection was—as the panel tried to guess it. Guests could win a whopping $150 provided by "the good folks at Borden."

In Keaton's appearance, the only man who ever hit him with a cream pie in a movie was the guest (Keaton normally creaming others). The panel quickly guessed the connection, and so Rayburn and Keaton went into a lengthy and poorly executed "bit" where presumably Rayburn was to end up with pie in his face. It didn't work out—and even Rayburn admitted on air that "I'm normally a funny guy, but not tonight."

Another episode fared even worse when a rather agitated J. Fred Muggs, the famous chimpanzee "mascot" from NBC's *Today Show*, showed up. Muggs was in no mood to sit behind a panel desk and patiently wait for the questions from the panel. Muggs repeatedly jumped from his handler's lap and onto the desk, pointing his butt at the camera and completely blocking out the view of the host—Rayburn.

In moments that the audience seemed to love, but likely made animal lover Betty cringe, Muggs' handler, Buddy Manilla basically wrestled with the chimp to force him into place on his lap. Manilla also chased Muggs around the game show set, in and out of the cameras, for several seconds as the chimp attempted to calm down. His "babysitter" was on the show as the "connection" guest. Rayburn eventually gave up and just revealed the connection between the guest and Muggs to the panel without any questions being asked.

In Love with Password

"A lot of wives tell me that their husbands are secretly in love with my wife," Ludden said on *The Merv Griffin Show*. "See, she's an old television star, she's been on since television was silent."[227]

Ludden said, "When Betty and Frank (Gifford) are on *Password* . . . the rating on *Password* goes as high as a 15 and 16 on daytime, and the share goes to a 55 and a 58. That means for those of us in the business, at that moment when Betty and Frank are on the show, we have a large, large bulk of the audience, and it is the highest rating that we have at any time during the year."[228]

During one episode of *Password*, Allen Ludden asked his wife Betty if she has a game playing philosophy:

"I love games, and I love game shows. I think it is a good mental exercise and keeps everyone alert and on their toes. You can't watch a game show without participating, and I think that's a good mental exercise for everybody, it doesn't matter how old or how young you are."

She adds, "And you meet a lot of husbands that way!"[229]

Betty said years later that she was proud that the Goodson-Todman shows she frequented went untouched by the game show scandals of early TV that ruined many careers.

In the early days of television, "the game shows got so very popular and the money got bigger and bigger, and they would get a good live contestant on, and unbeknownst to us (viewers), we all were rooting for them, but come to find out they were slipping answers to the good contestants," she said. "It never touched Goodson and Todman because you never could really win that much on their shows."[230]

Betty said Goodson-Todman ran "strictly honest shows" and because contestants weren't playing for that much money, the entertainment value was where the focus was. On the other shows—such as *21* or *The $64,000 Question*—"people got greedy, and it really did not help people's career."[231]

Match Game

If ever a game show broke all the rules—CBS' 1970s version of the popular *Match Game* was it. Created by the masters of game shows, Goodson and Todman, the show originally debuted on NBC way back in 1962. That version of the show, which also featured Betty as a panelist five times, was a cleaner, more respectable version than the later take on CBS. From 1962-69, NBC's version of *Match Game* was even played differently than the later version, with two teams of five contestants each led by celebrities who tried to get the most matches to the question possible. NBC tried to cancel the show in 1963, but changed their mind and it lasted another six years in daytime TV.

CBS revived *Match Game* for its daytime lineup in 1973 and hit game show gold—the show being a ratings success for six seasons. *Match Game* drifted so far from the game it was ultimately more fun to watch for what the panelists said than anything having to do with the actual game. Its success even spawned a successful night-time version, *Match Game P.M.* (presumably with even more adult content than the daytime version), that ran from 1975-82.

The daytime version was frequently paired with CBS' other successful daytime game, *Tattle Tales*, and allowed *Match Game* to showcase six A- and B-list celebrities together with host Gene Rayburn and two often-confused contestants. Rayburn's part was to keep it all running by reading questions such as, "Dumb Dora was so dumb, she put a (BLANK) in the oven."

Festooned in the best of 1970s music, costuming and set direction, *Match Game* may be right up there with *The Brady Bunch* as a show that best reflected the era in which it was produced. Funny, irreverent, and sometimes bawdy—*Match Game* seemed more like a collection of intelligent people having a few drinks at the local watering hole, than a game show.

Listed as a semi-regular, Betty appeared in dozens of episodes over the years, almost always seated in the sixth celebrity chair (front row, right) next to regular Richard Dawson (before his departure to his own hit game show, ABC's *Family Feud*). She admitted it was often the toughest spot to get a laugh out of—the other panelists usually stealing the best one-liners long before it was Betty's turn.

Regardless, Betty played well off regulars Brett Somers and Charles Nelson Reilly—often joining Charles in a well-placed putdown of Somers. Somers in return seemed to enjoy jabs pointed in Betty's direction. In total, Betty appeared on *Match Game* 26 times during the 1970s.

Betty was in good company as a "semi-regular" on the show—the other celebrities on that special list included Steve Allen, Patty Duke Astin, Orson Bean, Joyce Bulifant, Gary Burghoff, Bill Daily, Patti Deutsch, David Doyle, Fannie Flagg, Eva Gabor, Arte Johnson, Elaine Joyce, Lee Meriwether, Scoey Mitchell, Mary Ann Mobley, Nipsey Russell, Avery Schreiber, Debralee Scott, Marcia Wallace, and Mary Wickes.

Many regular viewers of *Match Game* then, and now, believed the loose nature of the celebrity panel reflected perhaps a liquid lunch. "People always say to me that they can spot an episode that was taped after lunch," Betty said. "They think there was all this booze. But there wasn't, we were just silly. It was a party all the time with a bunch of crazy people. We were funny without the booze."[232]

Ironically, it was the success of *Match Game* alumnus Richard Dawson on *Family Feud*, along with NBC's wildly popular new show, *Wheel of Fortune*, which spelled the end for *Match Game* (the last daytime episode airing on CBS in April 1979). *Match Game P.M.* continued on in syndication on independent and network affiliate stations until 1982, when it too, was canceled.

The show's popularity apparently remained; however, as NBC strangely tried to pair it with another game show standard, *Hollywood Squares,* for the confusing *Match Game-Hollywood Squares Hour* in 1983-84. ABC also took a stab at a revival in 1990-91 (Betty appearing in five of those episodes), and first-run syndicated versions of the show sold to stations in 1998-99.

On March 15, 2002, the *CBS Early Show* ran, as part of its "Retro Reunions" series a segment featuring Betty, Charles Nelson Reilly and Brett Somers. Somers said the best way to describe the show was "six people who didn't know what they're doing or saying, were not smart, put them on a panel, and find two contestants off the street and ask them dopey questions."[233]

Betty claimed—to hoots and hollers from Brett and Charles—that "I was the only dignified one on the show. I tried to bring a little class, but it just didn't work."[234]

Betty and Charles noted that the show wasn't scripted—it was all ad-libbed. "On *Match Game*, what you saw was what you got, we were out there without a net," Nelson Reilly said.[235]

Rayburn said he liked the loose nature of the '70s version—"it was a lousy format, we had to do something to liven it up."[236]

The taping schedule was grueling—sometimes as many as six half-hour shows in one day were taped at CBS Television City so that they would have episodes to use in the *Match Game P.M.* rotation.

Memorable Match Moments

Because it broke all the traditional "game show rules," *Match Game*, particularly its 1970s version on both daytime and evening schedules on CBS, provided some memorable moments.

In one episode, Betty appeared along with her husband, *Password* host Allen Ludden. During the "Super Match" round of the show, the contestant has called on two other celebrities, and for her third pick says, "I'll give Betty a try."

Host Gene Rayburn can't resist—and immediately jumps in with, "I've given Betty a try."

At that Ludden jumps from his seat and charges Rayburn in a fit of feigned jealous rage. Rayburn weakly adds, "It was just a joke, a pun."

For her part, Betty let her dimples do the talking and did what she was there to do—give the right answer winning $500 for the contestant.

In another funny moment, Betty offers the wrong answer to a question about what a mad scientist would get by crossing a girl and a hippopotamus. She says "big hips"—but the contestant has said "big butt." Betty protests the judge's ruling that she's wrong—thinking the hips are a part of the butt. The judges don't relent, but Gene helps demonstrate—with his hands on Betty's backside—the difference between hips and butt.

One question on the show concerned who Betty might have preferred to marry other than Ludden. The obvious answers were other game show hosts—such as Rayburn, Monty Hall or Art

Linkletter. Brett Somers got a big laugh by listing Charles Nelson Reilly's name. Betty herself didn't match, she listed King Kong.

"If I'd married him I wouldn't have to use the elevator, he could just lift me up to the fourth floor," Betty explained.

Other moments were racier—semi-regular Fannie Flagg wore a sparkling TV shirt that read across her ample breast, "This space for rent." Somers quickly chimed in with: "She's tired of giving it away!"

One contestant said he really, really wanted to kiss Fannie Flagg. Rayburn couldn't resist, and adds, "We get a lot of Fannie kissers on this show!"

Rayburn's raciest statement—a complete gaffe—was as he introduced a female contestant. Meaning to use the word "dimples," he declares: "Doesn't she have pretty nipples?!"

At age 90, Betty has outlived many of the *Match Game* regulars, including Gene Rayburn, Charles Nelson Reilly, Brett Somers, and Richard Dawson. Dawson, who went on to a long-running stint as host of the popular game show, *Family Feud*, died in June 2012. Upon his death, Betty reflected on all the good times on the *Match Game* set next to Dawson.

"We used to have such fun," she said. "Never give a celebrity a marker and a pen, because you get yourself in lots of trouble."[237]

Betty referred to Dawson as "Dickie" and noted, "He would draw ants across his card, and then across the table, and then across my card. And it wasn't just funny, but we thought it was the funniest thing in the world."[238]

JUST MEN!

In 1983, Betty finally succeeded in convincing network executives that a woman *could* successfully emcee a game show. It only took about 40 years! The show, *Just Men!* premiered on NBC daytime in January 1983.

"A woman emcee is not exactly my idea of heaven," Betty said. "My agents tried to sell me as a game show hostess 20 years ago and again 10 years ago without success. The networks said women at home want to look at men, not females. They also were convinced viewers were tired of hearing feminine voices, that they preferred the more authoritative male sounds."[239]

The basic premise of *Just Men!* was built for Betty (and really for her previous primetime alter-ego, Sue Ann Nivens). Two female contestants used prepared questions to pepper seven male "celebrities" in order to win a car. The male "celebrities" included regular primetime TV stars, but also a large sampling of daytime soap actors and professional athletes. Betty's job was to move between the men and do what she does so well— ad lib funny lines.

"Sue Ann (Nivens) would have gone bananas," Betty told reporters. "And I love every minute of the show myself."[240]

Betty even joked that she liked being at the center of the all-male panel so much, "I'm wracking my brain for a way to get rid of the women (contestants)," she said.[241]

As one reviewer put it, *Just Men!* "is not a hold-your-breath contest of intelligence, nor does it involve big bucks. It is, simply, a framework for a talk show."[242]

Despite the promising set-up, *Just Men!* began to lack a critical piece for success: Support from NBC executives. Several of them were open in their criticism of the show, and of Betty's performance on it—including friend Grant Tinker who felt the format did not showcase Betty's assets as a panelist and performer.

For some odd reason—for example—the show's producers had Betty running around the set from desk-to-desk asking the questions and holding microphones in front of celebrities. The show never tried the "emcee at a podium" approach that was tried and true in TV game shows.

Four months into *Just Men!* NBC canceled the show in April 1983 after taping 65 episodes, replacing it with another short-lived game show, *The New Battlestars*, hosted by Alex Trebec.

Life With Elizabeth

Lest anyone be confused—Betty's early TV career had a lot more going for it than game shows. In fact, Betty White is a part of TV history.

Although Lucille Ball is often credited as one of TV's first pioneering women, Betty may have beat Lucy to the starting line. In 1953, she and producer Don Fedderson took her "Life with Elizabeth" skits from her daytime TV show and expanded them into full, 30-minute sit-com episodes. Wisely, Fedderson and White (who co-produced the show) filmed each episode using three cameras—creating perhaps TV's first potential reruns (again, an invention credited to Lucy and Desi Arnaz, Sr. for their early films of CBS' mega-hit, *I Love Lucy*).

The "Life with Elizabeth" sketches were always set up by one of three songs Betty would sing in Fedderson's show. "Don called us into the office and said, 'That husband and wife thing you do on the show, do you think you could make that into a half-hour series?'"[243]

"I was worried that we could make a half hour out of that," Betty said. "I thought the jokes wouldn't hold on that long."[244]

The "Life with Elizabeth" skits were part of the very first *Betty White Show*, first broadcast locally in southern California by KLAC-TV, and later on NBC as a daytime show. It was standard daytime TV fare for its day—Betty reading note cards with jokes submitted by viewers (minus a studio audience, the jokes sort of fell flat with no one really laughing), and even Monday as "Wish Day" where wishes for children from one of "the local children's homes around Los Angeles" were granted.

Show segments included Betty setting up sponsor ads—for combating "tired blood" with Geritol or "reducing" with R-D-X weight loss pills. Betty opened each episode singing a familiar tune: "It's time to say, hello again! And start our show again! And sing a song or two for all of you!"

The first *Betty White Show* was also significant for its prominent feature of one of television's first African-American stars—Arthur Duncan. The show also featured a small in-studio orchestra led by Frank DeVol.

Opening to the strains of a harp, the filmed series version of *Life with Elizabeth* featured three anecdotal stories to each episode—three separate small stories—rather than a linear story that ran through a full 30-minute episode. Story lines were familiar—and predictable—Elizabeth's character wanting money for a new dress, or thinking up a new scheme.

"I wondered whether a full-half hour would work," Betty said. "A lot I knew! Funny thing, since then the half-hour situation comedy has done pretty well, eh?"[245]

Life with Elizabeth started out as a syndicated show sold directly to TV stations across the country, but eventually was picked up by NBC for its national schedule. The show was produced twice each week, both times in front of a live audience. The first take was with an audience to test and gauge their reactions to the jokes. The second audience was used mostly for a laugh track, or to pick up and improve scenes that didn't work the first time.

"We had a $1.95 budget with no sets or scenes," Betty said. "Lucy came along and (she and Desi) really knew how to do it. Lucy sort of had the idea that a half-hour situation comedy would work—and I think she did rather well, don't you?"[246]

Irrespective of its tiny budget and lackluster support from audiences and critics at times, *Life with Elizabeth* remains an important standard-bearer in early television history. Because of

Betty's role as co-creator and executive producer, she became the first woman to play a major role in controlling her own on-screen persona. Lucy may have worked closely with Desi as part of their DesiLu empire, but it was Betty who was in the front office slightly before Lucy.

Beyond the budgetary challenges forcing the show to want for elaborate sets or scenes, it also taught Betty a lot about how to ad lib. She recalls one episode in which she and co-star Del Moore both forgot their lines in a restaurant scene. Moore jumped up from the booth and excused himself (to go off stage and refresh himself on his lines).

"So, I'm left there alone, so I start to play with the salt and peppers, and I build a little house with the knives and forks," Betty said. "I thought (Del) was never going to come back. The audience is sitting there expectantly thinking that something marvelous is going to happen, and I think this has got to be the end of the world, this is the worse thing that has ever happened to me."[247]

The show ended its original run in 1955, two years after its start, but not before winning Betty her first Emmy Award—and creating a long line of reruns that ran for many years on TV stations across the U.S.

A Date with the Angels

Date with the Angels represented the first of several attempts at situation comedies for Betty, airing on Friday nights on ABC from May to December 1957 and lasting one additional month on Wednesday nights in January 1958 before it finally ended, filming 33 episodes.

One of many "domestic comedies" popping up on all three networks following the break-out success of Lucille Ball and Desi Arnaz on CBS' *I Love Lucy*, *Date with the Angels* cast Betty as a new bride Vickie Angel and her new husband Gus Angel, played by veteran actor Bill Williams. Williams, who had previously worked with Betty in radio and in local TV, played an insurance salesman who like Arnaz was witness to his wife's schemes with an assortment of neighbors and friends serving as the foils.

Also like Lucy, it was a production of the Ball-Arnaz success story, DesiLu Studios. Hollywood veteran Don Fedderson produced the show with Betty—Fedderson would have bigger success, however, with some of his other shows, including *My Three Sons*, *Family Affair*, and *The Lawrence Welk Show*. The show was heavily promoted by the Plymouth Motor Car Company, and featured Plymouth vehicles in the opening and closing credits.

The show had promise—but Betty was concerned that it lacked "that certain something," in part because Williams was not suited to the role of a comic sidekick. Williams had scored well as a lead for four seasons in an earlier ABC western, *The Adventures of Kit Carson*.

"Thirteen weeks into it, we realized Bill was not a comedian," Betty said. "After Dell Moore on *Life with Elizabeth* who was funny and our chemistry was great together, we decided that Bill was not going to work, so we stopped doing *Date with the Angels* and spent the last 13 weeks doing sketches with guest stars."

ABC let Betty keep the same time slot, but renamed the show *The Betty White Show*. It was the first network iteration of a show bearing her name—but wouldn't be the last.

The show consisted of two or three skits each week with a variety of guest stars, including actors Charles Coburn and Billy De Wolfe. Teen actor Jimmy Boyd, who had occasional appearances on *Date with the Angels*, also showed up on *The Betty White Show*. It didn't matter—Betty's new effort fared no better than *Date with the Angels*, and ratings-starved ABC finally canceled the series for good in April 1958.

Late Nights with Jack

Betty White was really never too far away from a camera, if ever. But after *Date with the Angels* ended, she kept busy during regular shots on other shows—most especially NBC's *Tonight Show* hosted by Jack Paar.

"Being on the Jack Paar program was just wonderful, and he was just wonderful," Betty said. "He invited me to come back, and I appeared on over 70 shows."[248]

Betty said she learned a lot from Paar, a pioneer of the talk show genre.

"Watching him work and working with him, as talk shows went on, staffs of people would interview the guests and write down the questions for the host to ask. It was all sort of pre-digested before you went on the air," Betty said. "Not with Paar. You'd be in makeup and you'd be panicking about what he was going to ask you . . . whatever came into his mind. It was exciting, you had to stay on your toes."[249]

Paar was so successful, she believes, because "he listened to his guests, that was the key, and he based his questions off of what his guests said, so that is why it worked. It was really excellent television."[250]

The Tonight Show appearances kept her in front of NBC executives as well who asked her to come to New York and audition for a regular spot on their morning franchise vehicle, *The Today Show.* Partly because doing so would mean leaving Los Angeles and living in New York, Betty said no. NBC went with a young Barbara Walters instead.

"My decisions were not all wise, but they were done with convictions," she said.[251]

9

Betty: The Animals & The Audience

If you want to understand why Betty stays active in television and films at her age, you may want to consider what it means to her to support her favorite animal causes. "I always say, I have to stay in show business to pay for my animal business," Betty said.[252]

She also clarifies what she sees her role as being: "I'm not into animal rights at all," Betty said. "I am into animal health and welfare."[253]

A volunteer with the Los Angeles Zoo for more than 15 years, Betty is also highly committed to the Morris Animal Foundation, which she describes as an animal health organization. "We fund humane studies into specific health problems of dogs, cats, horses, and zoo wildlife," she said. "We helped develop the feline leukemia vaccine and the parvovirus vaccine for dogs and the Potomac fever vaccine for horses. It's a wonderful organization."[254]

For her 90th birthday, Betty's co-stars on *Hot in Cleveland* adopted an elephant orphaned in Africa by ivory hunters. It was a perfect gift.[255]

Betty loves the animals, as this 2008 photo of Betty and her at-home pals can attest. *(PR Newswire/ Morris Animal Foundation)*

The gift made perfect sense to anyone paying attention—Betty is in love with the animals. The American Humane Society sees it that way as well, honoring Betty with their National Humanitarian Medal and Legacy Award during an expensive, and glitzy fundraising gala at the Beverly Hilton Hotel in October 2012.

The award and a chance to help raise funds for the American Humane Society was an easy call for Betty. "I got involved in this terrific charity 60 years ago because of our shared commitment to the welfare of animals," she said. "As an actor, I saw first-hand the crucial work the American Humane Society was doing to protect animals in entertainment through their 'No Animals Were Harmed' certification program, which has kept more than a million of our most beloved co-stars safe on set."[256]

Betty also signed up for the Hero Dog Awards TV special planned by the American Humane Society—designed to honor working dogs that have made a difference in the lives of humans.

It seems Betty gets pulled into the act, even when she's not involved, as is the case with the Capron Park Zoo in Attleboro, Massachusetts. In 2012, the zoo obtained a rare "white alligator" for display. The "white" or albino alligator is known often as a "swamp ghost" for its unusual color. And what did the good folks at the Capron Zoo do? They named the female alligator "Betty White"—just one of 200 known albino gators to exist in the world.

Later that same year, Betty drew a crowd to the zoo, but this time it was actually her appearing in person, not an alligator bearing her name. At the National Zoo in Washington, D.C., Betty got a rare behind-the-scenes tour of the facility and met briefly with some fans.

"Whenever I travel, I try to steal time to check out whatever zoo is within reach" Betty said in her new book, *Betty & Friends: My Life at the Zoo*. At the National Zoo, Betty fed a 14-year-old giant panda bear, visited the bird house display and met a gorilla.

The National Zoo was excited to have not only a celebrity, but a true friend to the animals in their presence. Their blog boasted, "she held a tiny lemur leap frog, she admired some Japanese giant salamanders and visited with the elephants . . . she was even introduced to 'Rose,' the zoo's Cuban crocodile named after her *Golden Girls* character, Rose Nylund."[257]

The Morris Foundation and L.A. Zoo

Betty's work with animals has extended into her life off-camera as well. Her work with the nationally respected Morris Animal Foundation for Wildlife became even more important during the devastating effects of the 2010 British Petroleum oil spill disaster in the Gulf of Mexico. The foundation formed the "Betty White Wildlife Rapid Response Fund" to respond to natural disasters and emerging diseases among animals. For the Gulf disaster, Betty said she would personally match all donations to the effort up to $25,000.

"The need is so great right now," Betty said, as weeks passed by and thousands upon thousands of oil burped into the gulf. For Betty, the "Rapid Response Fund" was one of more than 30 studies she had helped fund through the Denver-based Morris Foundation.

Betty served as president emeritus of the Morris Foundation after having given more than 40 years of volunteer time and donations to the cause. In 1987, the American Veterinary Medical Association awarded Betty its Humane Award in 1987.

A trustee with the Morris Foundation since 1971, Betty also served as a trustee of the Greater Los Angeles Zoo Association, including eight years as a member of the board of commissioners for the zoo. In 2006, the City of Los Angeles installed a special plaque next to the gorilla cage at the L.A. Zoo naming Betty, "Ambassador to the Animals."

"Half my life is working in a profession I love, and the other half is working with animals. I couldn't ask for more," Betty said.[258]

That "other half" of her life—TV and movie roles—kept her in front of the camera despite any setback she experienced.

THE PET SET

One effort (though a ratings failure) involved Betty's effort to combine her love of animals with her love of TV. Betty hosted 39 episodes of *The Pet Set*, a nationally syndicated talk show with celebrities and their pets (coming on the air in 1970, and leaving almost as quickly in 1971).

Betty wrote and produced all 39 episodes and recalled Rod Serling's appearance with his Irish setter "Mitch" as among the most interesting guests on the show. But Serling was just the start of the parade of stars that appeared, including Doris Day, Mary Tyler Moore, Lorne Greene, James Brolin, Jimmy Stewart, Michael Landon, Bob Barker, and Peter Lawford.

The show was based on showcasing a celebrity and their pet. The show was written by Betty and tried to focus mostly on the star's interest in animals. Producing *The Pet Set* was a natural fit for Betty.

"My parents were so disappointed that I only had two legs and no tail . . . my parents were even bigger animal lovers than me," she said.[259]

Although love of animals came naturally, the White household was not crawling with critters. "We always had to try to keep it down to about three (pets) because you run out of hands," Betty said. "And the close relationships—if you have too many animals you don't get that wonderful one-on-one relationship."[260]

Her closest relationship in her later years was with her beloved golden retriever Pontiac—an animal she dubbed "a career change guide dog."[261]

While dogs have remained near the center of Betty's heart always, *The Pet Set* featured more than just household pets. All types of animals—elephants, water buffalo, and dogs and cats were included. The show, however, was not done in front of an audience, perhaps contributing to its rather flat presentation at times. Betty recalled, however, one lively show with five lions on one show—and no "bathroom" accidents ever on the show.

A ratings failure, but a personal success, Betty declared *The Pet Set* among "the happiest I've ever been on television."

What Others Say About Betty

"She is an eclectic lady and she is a renaissance woman," Edward Asner, "Lou Grant" from *The Mary Tyler Moore Show*, said. "She can sense her audience. She knows what will work. She knows how to stop. And she knows how to top. She's a master at all of those."

MTM's *Rhoda* star Valerie Harper noted that it was "Tina Turner showed women how to dance in heels . . . I said, 'Betty White shows us how to be a star.'"[262]

Betty gets cozy at the February 2012 premiere of Universal Studios production, *Dr. Suess' The Lorax.* *(Shutterstock.com/ Phil Stafford)*

Gavin MacLeod, "Murray Slaughter" on the original Moore show (and later Captain Merrill Stubing on *The Love Boat*) had many on-screen moments with Betty. He believes her to be a national treasure. "There's something about Betty, no matter what roles she plays, you're intrigued," MacLeod said.[263]

Mary Tyler Moore, Betty's long-time friend and major benefactor via her hilarious appearances on Mary's historic CBS sitcom noted that there is something very memorable about Betty. "She can be both tender and sweet, and empathetic to people who are going through times that are tough. She can be just outrageously funny and get you out of a blue mood. She's a very special woman."[264]

Rue McClanahan said, "Whenever I think of Betty White, I always see her big, open smile. I always said Betty had those little Orphan Annie eyes, you know, those hollow eyes with nothing in them. I thought she was so funny in the part of

Rose. Betty and I were acutely aware that we were part of this wonderful, wonderful show and that it might not happen again (in our careers). Every day was golden, and every week went by just like that!"[265]

Estelle Getty said, "Betty White has been in television as long as anyone can remember, and as long as she can remember. She very often says she was famous in silent television."

Getty added, "She is a good person, she's good people. I know she is adored by her fans, and that must be a bit of a burden, but she is adored."

And Getty said Betty's Emmy win over the rest of the cast of *The Golden Girls* during the show's first season never caused a problem. "I suppose that could be hard to take when you've won something that is coveted by other people, and they haven't. You won it, and want it, and you want them to be happy too," Getty said.

"Betty White has logged more hours on television, I think than any other human being, ever," said Mary Tyler Moore.[266]

Moore added, "She is such a good actress that you very quickly forget any personal reality that you have, you just get into the character and the scene and its premise. I didn't spend much time saying, 'Good for you Betty' because I was just focused on laughing at one of her St. Olaf stories or whatever she was doing."

Another comedy legend, Carol Burnett, remembers well Betty's guest appearances during her successful 11-year run on CBS' *The Carol Burnett Show*. Asked about Betty backstage at the January 2011 NBC gala for Betty's 90th birthday, Burnett offered that, "Betty was always on time. She would always know her lines, but sometimes she would change them and make them funnier. She also would remember every crewmember's name, every time. She's funny, she's bawdy, she sings, she's a great actress, and a good friend."[267]

Former Los Angeles Mayor Richard J. Riordan, a Republican, has known Betty throughout her years in Hollywood. "Betty came to Los Angeles when she was two-years-old, she went through school here, and has been an integral part of our community for years. She's always been someone who has been willing to get her hands dirty. At the zoo, she's always there. The secret to being happy in life is to be a giver. And no one is a bigger giver than Betty White. Nobody is happier than Betty White."[268]

Tippi Hedren, actress and president of the Roar Foundation, says Betty's "eyes always light up when she talks about the animals, and when she talks about her own animals."[269]

These days her co-stars on TV Land's breakout hit, *Hot in Cleveland*, have equally praiseworthy words. Co-star Wendie Malick said, "We just have so much gratitude about being with her and with each other. It's a very fun show."[270]

Another co-star, Valerie Bertinelli adds, "Working with Betty is like having a master class in comedy. She gets it, it's just a gift. Now she's honed (her talent) over quite a few years, but she starts with that gift of comedy."[271]

BETTY ON BETTY

During a memorable 2008 appearance on the daytime *Bonnie Hunt Show*, Betty discussed her earliest days in TV— also in daytime.

"The most we ever did was 54 commercials in one day," she said. "They would hand you these typed up cards and you'd never seen it before. But you'd read it and sell your heart out. It was like going to Television College."[272]

Betty admitted she's not a fan of everything on TV. She told Hunt that she's "not into" reality TV shows and that "I don't watch that much TV anymore. I don't have much time."

Hunt asked a pointed question, "Have you ever done a nude scene?"[273]

Betty replied: "Well, people thought it was. It was in *Annie's Point*, a Hallmark film. My granddaughter and I were swimming and we shot the scene at 3 o'clock in the morning . . . and the water was supposed to be warm. It was ice cold . . . it wasn't my most convincing acting ever."[274]

Pat Sajak, on his short-lived CBS late night show, *The Pat Sajak Show*, noted that Betty typically played parts that matched her age and didn't go in for "all sorts of nips and tucks." His sideways reference to plastic surgery only prompted a funny line from Betty (without admitting whether she'd ever had any): "Well, gravity does take over at some point."[275]

In the same interview, however, she later admits to having work done on her eyelids in 1977 as part of preparing for *The Betty White Show*.

"I have such good health, I'm the healthiest one around, but I'm chicken, that's what I am," she said. "I have a very low pain threshold. But unless it is surgery that is necessary for your health, I just don't have the courage to have it. I have heard so many horror stories about cosmetic surgery. You can't hold back the hands of time for too long."[276]

In receiving the 2009 Lifetime Achievement Award from the Screen Actors' Guild—the award for the actor who fosters "the finest ideals of the acting profession," SAG National President Alan Rosenburg said, "Whether creating some of television's most indelible characters, plunging into film roles with joyous gusto or perfecting the art of the quip as a television panelist and host, Betty White has entertained audiences with her impeccable comic timing and remarkable wit for more than 60 years. Her lifelong devotion to the welfare of the animals, manifest in her work as an author, producer and philanthropist, is further evidence of her tremendous humanity and meaningful contributions in so many important areas."[277]

While humbled, Betty admits "I don't even know that I will be remembered. I would just like to have it that my life, the animal part and the television part, I worked them together as much as I could. By doing all the game shows, talk shows, and the sitcoms, all the diversity . . . the audience has taken it that Betty is a good friend of theirs that they like to invite into their home."[278]

Betty likes to spend as much time at her home in Carmel, California, "as much as I possibly can, which seems to be getting less and less, with my golden retriever Pontiac. He's a career-trained guide dog, but I like to think of him as the Indian chief, not the car."[279]

Time at home, usually spent alone, means Betty is deep into one of her daily crossword puzzles, and of course, needlepoint.

The Meaning of Life

After nine decades of life, Betty has experienced more than her share of loss. Both of her parents and her beloved Allen Ludden all preceded her in death. To her surprise, despite being the oldest *Golden Girl*, she's outlived the entire cast. In 2011, appearing on *The Joy Behar Show* on HLN, she was asked about whether she thinks about death or dying.

"My mother had the most wonderful approach to death," Betty said. "She always said, 'We know so many things. We know almost everything there is to know in the world, but we don't know what happens at that moment (of death).' She said, 'So whenever we lose somebody, we know, now they know the secret.'"[280]

Betty believes in an afterlife—but goes for the joke when she adds that an afterlife "would be interesting, provided that I earned the privilege of what I do and where I go!"[281]

Humor seeps in even in serious topics like death—Betty even appeared on CBS' *The Late Show with David Letterman* to offer her own special Top Ten list: "Betty White's Top Ten Tips for a Long and Happy Life":

10 ... Get at least eight hours of beauty sleep, nine if you're ugly.

9 ... Exercise. Or don't! What the hell do I care?

8 ... Never apologize. It shows weakness.

7 ... The best way to earn a quick buck is a slip and fall lawsuit.

6 ... Avoid tweeting any photos of your private parts.

5 ... Schedule a nightly appointment with Dr. Johnny Walker.

4 ... Take some wheat grass, some soy paste, and a carob. Toss 'em in the garbage, and cut yourself a big ass piece of pork.

3 ... Try not to die.

2 ... Never dwell on past mistakes—especially you, LeBron (James).

... And her No. 1 tip for living a long life? Don't waste your time watching this crap.[282]

No one should be surprised that Betty goes for a laugh when talking about the key to a long life. "Laughter and good health, how many 90-year-olds are feeling as good as I am?" Betty asks. "Good health gives you the energy to be able to do things. Believe me, I'm always in deep surprise that I'm still feeling good enough to look forward to stuff."[283]

Betty said she learned at her mother's knee that "you take each day at a time, keep your sense of humor, God knows you need it. But I'm 90 and a half, and it just gets better . . . and I can get away with murder at this age. Everybody spoils you rotten . . . and I never take it for granted."[284]

Endnotes

Ch. 1 • Senior Moments

1   *People* magazine, Aug. 25, 2012
2   Ibid.
3   WBBM-TV, Chicago, June 13, 2012
4   *Washington Post*, May 12, 2012;
     Associated Press, May 12, 2012
5   HuffingtonPost.com, June 12, 2012
6   *Variety* magazine, Aug. 23, 2012
7   Entertainment Weekly.com,
     June 17, 2010
8   *New York Magazine*, May 9, 2010
9   American Comedy Awards, 1987
10 Ibid.
11 *New York Magazine*, May 24, 2010
12 *Shoot*, July 16, 2010
13 Ibid.
14 Ibid.
15 *Inside the Actors Studio*, Sept. 28, 2010
16 *New York Daily News*, Sept. 26, 2012
17 *Advertising Age*, Aug. 8, 2012
18 Consumerreports.com, Aug. 3, 2012
19 *New York Times*, Aug. 2, 2012
20 Ibid.
21 *Pittsburgh Post-Gazette*, May 5, 2010
22 Ibid.
23 Ibid.
24 Ibid.
25 *New York Magazine*, May 9, 2010
26 *Saturday Night Live*, NBC, May 8, 2010
27 Ibid.
28 Ibid.
29 *Inside the Actors Studio*, Sept. 28, 2010
30 Ibid.
31 American Academy of Television Arts
     and Sciences, news web site entry,
     April 30, 2010
32 *Hollywood Reporter*, Sept. 15, 2009
33 American Academy interview,
     EmmyTVLegends.com
34 Ibid.
35 *Wall Street Journal*, June 13, 2012
36 Sheknowsparenting.com, Aug. 6, 2012
37 *USA Today*, May 3, 2012
38 *Washington Post*, Sept. 22, 2012
39 *The Canadian Press*, Aug. 5, 2012

Ch. 2 • White Hot

40 Entertainment Weekly.com,
     June 17, 2010
41 *PaleyFest: Inside the Media*,
     March 8, 2011
42 Ibid.
43 Ibid.
44 *Hot in Cleveland*, pilot episode,
     June 16, 2010
45 *Inside the Actors Studio*, Sept. 28, 2010
46 Ibid.
47 HuffingtonPost.com, June 15, 2010
48 Ibid.
49 Ibid.
50 *Kathy Griffin: My Life on the 'D List'*,
     Bravo, July 6, 2009
51 *New York Post*, May 18, 2012
52 CNN Entertainment Blog, May 18, 2012
53 *New York Post*, May 18, 2012
54 ABCNews.com, June 15, 2010
55 Ibid.
56 Ibid.
57 CNN Entertainment Blog, Aug. 8, 2012
58 *PaleyFest: Inside the Media*,
     March 8, 2011
59 Ibid.
60 Ibid.
61 Associated Press, Aug. 20, 2012
62 *Hollywood Reporter*, June 7, 2010
63 Ibid.
64 *Lopez Tonight*, TBS, 2010
65 CNN Entertainment Blog, Aug. 8, 2012
66 Ibid.

Ch. 3 • Life with Betty

67 *Late Show with David Letterman*, CBS,
     May 4, 2011

68   American Academy interview, EmmyTVLegends.com

69   Ibid.

70   American Academy interview, EmmyTVLegends.com

71   Ibid.

72   Ibid.

73   Ibid.

74   Ibid.

75   Ibid.

76   Ibid.

77   *Lifetime Intimate Portrait*, Season 6, Episode 6, 1993

78   Ibid.

79   Ibid.

80   Ibid.

81   *TV Magazine*, April 16, 1989

82   *Lifetime Intimate Portrait*, Season 6, Episode 6, 1993

83   Ibid.

84   *TV Magazine*, April 16, 1989

85   *Toronto Star*, Jan. 19, 1986

86   Ibid.

87   *This Is Your Life: Betty White*, 1987

88   Ibid.

89   *TV Magazine*, April 16, 1989

90   *Inside the Actors Studio*, Bravo, Sept. 28, 2010

91   *Lifetime Intimate Portrait*, Season 6, Episode 6, 1993

92   Ibid.

93   Ibid.

94   Ibid.

95   *Barbara Walters Special*, ABC, Dec. 2, 1986

96   Canfield, J. (1998). *Chicken Soup for the Pet Lover's Soul*. Deerfield Beach, FL: Health Communications.

97   American Academy interview, EmmyTVLegends.com

98   *Inside the Actors Studio*, Bravo, Sept. 28, 2010

99   Associated Press, Oct. 8, 1980

100 Associated Press, Oct. 13, 17, and 29, 1980; Nov. 3, 1980

101 *TV Magazine*, April 16, 1989

102 Associated Press, Jan. 8, 1981

103 Ibid.

104 Associated Press, June 9, 1981

105 *Barbara Walters Special*, ABC, Dec. 2, 1986

106 *TV Magazine*, April 16, 1986

107 *Lifetime Intimate Portrait*, Season 6, Episode 6, 1993

108 Associated Press, June 9, 1981

109 *TV Magazine*, April 16, 1989

110 Canfield, J. (1998). *Chicken Soup for the Pet Lover's Soul*. Deerfield Beach, FL: Health Communications.

111 *Barbara Walters Special*, ABC, Dec. 2, 1986

112 United Press International, March 31, 1988

113 Ibid.

114 *TV Magazine*, April 16, 1989

115 Ibid.

116 *The Bonnie Hunt Show* , Oct. 27, 2008

117 *Inside the Actors Studio*, Bravo, Sept. 28, 2010

Ch. 4 • From *Mary* to *Mama*

118 *Hollywood Reporter*, Jan. 21, 2010

119 Ibid.

120 *Lifetime Intimate Portrait*, Season 6, Episode 6, 1993

121 Ibid.

122 Ibid.

123 Ibid.

124 Castleman, H., & Podrazik, W.J. (2003). *Watching TV: Six Decades of American Television*. Syracuse, NY: Syracuse University Press

125 Dow, B.J. (1996). *Primetime Feminism: Television, Media Culture, and the Women's Movement*. Philadelphia: University of Pennsylvania Press.

126 Ibid.

127 Ibid.

128 American Academy interview, EmmyTVLegends.com

129 Ibid.

130 Ibid.

131 Ibid.

132 Castleman, H., & Podrazik, W.J. (2003). *Watching TV: Six Decades of American Television*. Syracuse, NY: Syracuse University Press

133 American Academy interview, EmmyTVLegends.com

134 American Academy of Television Arts and Sciences web blog, April 30, 2010

135 Ibid.

136 *Toronto Star*, Jan. 19, 1986.

137 *The Mary Tyler Moore Show: 25th Anniversary Special*, CBS, February 1991

138 Castleman, H., & Podrazik, W.J. (2003). *Watching TV: Six Decades of American Television*. Syracuse, NY: Syracuse University Press

139 Kubey, R.W. (2004). *Creating Television: Conversations with People behind 50 Years of American Television*. Mahweh, NJ: Lawrence Erlbaum and Associates.

140 Tucker, D.C. (2007). *The Women Who Made Television Funny: Ten Stars of 1950s Sitcoms*. Jefferson, NC: McFarland & Company, Inc., Publishers.

141 Karol, M. (2004). *Funny Ladies: Sitcom Queens*. Lincoln, NE: iUniverse, Inc.

142 *Fritz's Night Owl Theatre*, undated KLAC-TV 1977 broadcast

143 Kubey, R.W. (2004). *Creating Television: Conversations with People behind 50 Years of American Television*. Mahweh, NJ: Lawrence Erlbaum and Associates.

144 Castleman, H., & Podrazik, W.J. (2003). *Watching TV: Six Decades of American Television*. Syracuse, NY: Syracuse University Press

145 Kubey, R.W. (2004). *Creating Television: Conversations with People behind 50 Years of American Television*. Mahweh, NJ: Lawrence Erlbaum and Associates.

146 Castleman, H., & Podrazik, W.J. (2003). *Watching TV: Six Decades of American Television*. Syracuse, NY: Syracuse University Press

147 American Academy interview, EmmyTVLegends.com

148 *The Bonnie Hunt Show*, Oct. 27, 2008

149 *Dean Martin Celebrity Roast: Betty White*, NBC, August 1978

Ch. 5 • The Golden Years

150 Associated Press, July 22, 1985

151 *New York Times*, Sept. 22, 1985

152 Associated Press, July 22, 1985

153 Ibid.

154 *New York Times*, Sept. 22, 1985

155 Ibid.

156 Ibid.

157 Colucci, J. (2006). *The Q Guide to the Golden Girls*. New York: Alyson Books.

158 *Lifetime Intimate Portrait*, Season 6, Episode 6, 1993

159 Colucci, J. (2006). *The Q Guide to the Golden Girls*. New York: Alyson Books.

160 Ibid.

161 Ibid.

162 Ibid.

163 Ibid.

164 *Barbara Walters Special*, ABC, Dec. 2, 1986

165 Ibid.

166 Ibid.

167 *New York Times*, Sept. 22, 1985

168 Ibid.

169 *Toronto Star*, Jan. 19, 1986

170 Ibid.

171 Ibid.

172 *Lifetime Intimate Portrait*, Season 6, Episode 6, 1993

173 Colucci, J. (2006). *The Q Guide to the Golden Girls*. New York: Alyson Books.

174 Ibid.

175 Ibid.

176 *Lifetime Intimate Portrait*, Season 6, Episode 6, 1993

177 *Barbara Walters Special*, ABC, Dec. 2, 1986

178 HuffingtonPost.com, June 12, 2012

Ch. 6 • A Rose By Any Other Name

179 *Lifetime Intimate Portrait*, Season 6, Episode 6, 1993
180 Ibid.
181 Ibid.
182 Colucci, J. (2006). *The Q Guide to the Golden Girls*. New York: Alyson Books.
183 Ibid.
184 Golden Girls DVD preview
185 *Lifetime Intimate Portrait*, Season 6, Episode 6, 1993
186 Ibid.
187 Ibid.
188 *Pittsburgh Post-Gazette*, May 5, 2010
189 Ibid.
190 *Lifetime Intimate Portrait*, Season 6, Episode 6, 1993
191 Ibid.
192 Ibid.
193 Ibid.
194 American Academy interview, EmmyTVLegends.com
195 Colucci, J. (2006). *The Q Guide to the Golden Girls*. New York: Alyson Books.
196 *San Diego Union-Tribune*, Nov. 18, 1991
197 American Academy interview, EmmyTVLegends.com
198 McClanahan, R. (2007). *My First Five Husbands: And the Ones Who Got Away*. New York: Broadway Books/ Random House.
199 *Inside Edition*, July 23, 2008
200 Ibid.
201 Ibid.
202 IMDB News, Aug. 7, 2008
203 Ibid.
204 Colucci, J. (2006). *The Q Guide to the Golden Girls*. New York: Alyson Books.
205 *Entertainment Tonight*, April 29, 2009
206 *ABC World News Tonight*, April 27, 2009
207 *TV Examiner,* June 3, 2010
208 Colucci, J. (2006). *The Q Guide to the Golden Girls*. New York: Alyson Books.

Ch. 7 • Moving On From Miami

209 CNN Transcript, *Larry King Live*, Sept. 15, 1995
210 Ibid.
211 *The Bonnie Hunt Show*, Oct. 27, 2008
212 *The Tonight Show Starring Johnny Carson*, 1987
213 Ibid.
214 WENN Entertainment News Wire, May 20, 2010
215 Ibid.
216 Ibid.
217 *The Pat Sajak Show*, CBS, Feb. 26, 1990
218 Ibid.
219 *New York Magazine*, June 16, 2010
220 *DVM Newsmagazine*, Sept. 27, 2012
221 Ibid.
222 Ibid.

Ch. 8 • Fun And Games With Betty

223 *Toronto Star*, Jan. 19, 1986
224 Ibid.
225 *This Is Your Life: Betty White*, 1987
226 Ibid.
227 *The Merv Griffin Show*, undated tape, 1966
228 Ibid.
229 *Password* episode 1555, NBC, undated
230 American Academy interview, EmmyTVLegends.com
231 Ibid.
232 Game Show Network Live, Aug. 1, 2008
233 *CBS Early Show*, March 15, 2002
234 Ibid.
235 Ibid.
236 *The Maury Povich Show*, undated clip
237 People.com, June 4, 2012
238 Ibid.
239 United Press International, March 7, 1983
240 Ibid.
241 Ibid.
242 Ibid.
243 *Inside the Actors Studio*, Bravo, Sept. 28, 2010

244 *Pioneers in Television*, PBS, March 22, 2011

245 Ibid.

246 Ibid.

247 Ibid.

248 American Academy interview, EmmyTVLegends.com

249 Ibid.

250 Ibid.

251 Ibid.

Ch. 9 • Betty: The Animals & The Audience

252 *Hinsdale* (Ill.) *Daily Herald*, Aug. 17, 2012

253 CNN Transcript, *Larry King Live*, Sept. 15, 1995

254 *Hinsdale* (Ill.) *Daily Herald*, Aug. 17, 2012

255 *PaleyFest: Inside the Media*, March 8, 2011

256 Starpulse.com, Sept. 25, 2012

257 National Zoo blog, May 18, 2012

258 *Hollywood Reporter*, Jan. 21, 2010

259 *Hinsdale* (Ill.) *Daily Herald*, Aug. 17, 2012

260 Ibid.

261 Ibid.

262 KABC-TV, Aug. 9, 2008

263 Ibid.

264 Artisan News Service, Jan. 16, 2011

265 *Lifetime Intimate Portrait*, Season 6, Episode 6, 1993

266 Ibid.

267 Artisan News Service, Jan. 16, 2011

268 *Lifetime Intimate Portrait*, Season 6, Episode 6, 1993

269 Ibid.

270 Artisan News Service, Jan. 16, 2011

271 Ibid.

272 American Academy interview, EmmyTVLegends.com

273 *The Bonnie Hunt Show*, Oct. 27, 2008

274 Ibid.

275 *The Pat Sajak Show*, CBS, Feb. 26, 1990

276 Ibid.

277 Screen Actors' Guild of America.

278 American Academy interview, EmmyTVLegends.com

279 EntertainmentTIME.com, Aug. 3, 2012

280 *The Joy Behar Show*, HLN, May 6, 2011

281 Ibid.

282 *Late Show with David Letterman*, CBS, June 13, 2011

283 *Houston Chronicle*, Sept. 25, 2012

284 Ibid.

Index